MUSIC FUN 101

101 Reproducible Music Games and Puzzles

by

Sue Albrecht Johnson

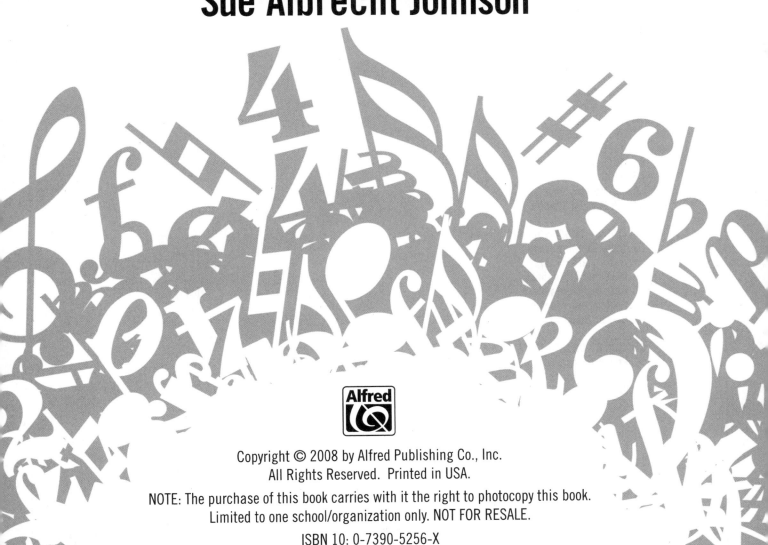

Alfred

ISBN 10: 0-7390-5256-X
ISBN 13: 978-0-7390-5256-3

CONTENTS

CONTENTS

	Page	Answer Key

SECTION 1 - ALPHAGRAMS

Place each of the featured letters of the alphabet once in the grid to form a word reading across in each line, fitting the Alphagram's theme. Some letters may fit in more than one of the empty squares to form a familiar word. However, only one arrangement of all the featured letters will complete the puzzle. These letters are provided in a box at the top of the Alphagram, so that each can be crossed out as it is used. A line is provided to write the name of the answer to the right of the grid.

TEACHER HINT: Four of the Alphagrams include an additional Word Search. Theses words all read across from left to right. An optional list of the additional words for those puzzles is included. In addition, some of these puzzles include matching exercises.

SECTION 2 - MATCHING PUZZLES

7. Match the composer to the work.
8.–9. Match the song to the musical.

SECTION 3 - NAME THAT TUNE

Match the song to the melody.

The Christmas Song puzzle utilizes primarily secular "winter songs." The Christmas Carol puzzle uses songs which have religious themes.

SECTION 4 - MUSICAL SUDOKU

This Sudoku is just like those using the digits 1 – 9. However, in this case you are using letters or symbols.

Complete the grid so each row, column and 3-by-3 box (in bold borders) contains every letter of the puzzle.

The puzzles get harder on each page. The teacher may give additional clues as desired.

SECTION 5 - CROSSWORDS

Four of the Crosswords are Treble or Bass Clef Crosswords. Instead of having clues written out, the clues are written as notes on a staff. The student is to find the letter of the note and write that in the puzzle.

The other two Crosswords involve completing the name of the Broadway musical and identifying terms used in the theater.

SECTION 6 - CRYPTO-LISTS

These are lists of related words and phrases that have been translated into simpler cipher alphabets. The letter substitutions remain constant within any on group of words. For example, if G represents A in one word, it will represent A in all the words in that list. The codes change from one list to the next. A tip for the students is to start thinking of answers that might fit one of the categories; then see if any words in the list have the same letter pattern. For younger students, the teacher may want to start by giving them a hint. (For example, "Every U in this puzzle represents an L.")

Teacher Hints:

64. Broadway Musicals: "THE" and "AND" are common words
65. Christmas Songs: U = L
66. Christmas Carols: E = N
67. Classical Composers: Includes the three B's
68. Modern Composers: John is a popular name
69. Musical Instruments: X = T
70. Songs by the Beatles: W = Y
71. Favorite Kids' Songs: Includes action songs; "THE" is used often
72. Patriotic Songs: I = A

SECTION 7 - MUSICAL CODES

These puzzles are a simpler form of Crypto-Lists. The code is given to the students. Their job is to substitute the given letter for each number. Dark squares indicate the end of a word.

SECTION 8 - SCRAMBLED WORDS

The object is to unscramble the letters to find a word or phrase that fits the puzzle theme. The answer is to be placed into the blocks in the right column. If there is a number underneath the letter, that letter should be placed in the numbered block at the bottom of the page. If done correctly, there will be bonus words formed at the bottom which also fit the theme of the puzzle.

SECTION 9 - WORD SEARCHES

These word searches have words going across (right to left and left to right), up and down, and diagonally.

SECTION 10 - KRISS KROSS

These puzzles are similar to crossword puzzles, except there are no numbers or clues. The object is to fit the words into the puzzle, either across or down, based on the number of letters. Be sure to work on musical vocabulary, spelling, and definitions with your students as they complete these puzzles. A starting hint is provided for each puzzle.

SECTION 11 - COMPLETE THE STORY

These stories incorporate several words which can be written on a staff. The student is to find the letters of the notes and translate those into words.

Students may also enjoy clapping or tapping the rhythms in these puzzles for the instructor. Keyboard classes may enjoy playing through these musical clues.

SECTION 12 - BUILDING BLOCKS

Imagine having 4 building blocks with one letter on each of the 6 sides. Then imagine trying to find out what words you can form using those blocks. In this case, you are given the words. The object is to figure out which letters appear on each block in order for this to work. For example, if one of the words is ALTO, the A would appear on one block, the L on a second block, the T on a third block, and the O on the fourth block.

SECTION 13 - BUILD-A-WORD

The object of Build-A-Word is to take one square from each column, left to right, in order to form words. You should be able to discover the name of the musical category. The other 4 words will which fit into that same category. Depending on the age group, you may need to give the students some kind of hint for the category.

SECTION 14 - MAZES (by Christopher Braden)

These mazes were created by the author's grandson, Christopher Braden, at age 14. Students may enjoy creating similar mazes in order to quiz each other. Feel free to trace just the outline of the piano or the maracas.

SECTION 1
ALPHAGRAMS

PUZZLE #1: BROADWAY MUSICALS

Fill in the blanks to form the name of a musical in each row, reading across. The name of the musical must include the letter that you put in the highlighted column. Use each letter of the alphabet once to complete the puzzle. (No J or X.)

NAME _____

A B C D E F G H I K L M N O P Q R S T U V W Y Z   MUSICALS

							▓							MUSICALS
1	S	O	U	N	D	O	▓	M	U	S	I	C	E	___
2	P	I	T	H	E	L	▓	O	D	O	L	L	Y	___
3	A	T	H	E	M	U	▓	I	C	M	A	N	Y	___
4	F	T	O	O	L	I	▓	E	R	C	R	E	W	___
5	I	D	O	I	D	O	▓	R	E	A	S	E	T	___
6	I	T	H	E	P	R	▓	D	U	C	E	R	S	___
7	T	I	S	H	O	W	▓	O	A	T	A	C	T	___
8	B	A	C	H	O	R	▓	S	L	I	N	E	R	___
9	W	E	S	T	S	I	▓	E	S	T	O	R	Y	___
10	D	A	N	C	E	C	▓	I	C	A	G	O	T	___
11	U	P	O	R	G	Y	▓	N	D	B	E	S	S	___
12	H	A	I	R	S	P	▓	A	Y	R	E	N	T	___
13	S	T	H	E	W	I	▓	P	I	P	P	I	N	___
14	C	A	T	H	E	L	▓	O	N	K	I	N	G	___
15	O	K	L	A	H	O	▓	A	K	E	U	P	S	___
16	O	F	F	U	N	N	▓	G	I	R	L	E	G	___
17	U	S	O	U	T	H	▓	A	C	I	F	I	C	___
18	A	S	C	O	R	E	▓	I	C	K	E	D	Y	___
19	K	I	S	S	M	E	▓	A	T	E	F	L	Y	___
20	S	C	U	E	V	I	▓	A	C	T	O	R	S	___
21	L	E	S	M	I	S	▓	R	A	B	L	E	S	___
22	C	A	N	C	A	N	▓	I	E	B	O	W	S	___
23	A	S	T	A	G	E	▓	A	B	A	R	E	T	___
24	A	V	E	N	U	E	▓	S	C	R	I	P	T	___

Can you find 5 other musicals and 14 other "show" terms hidden across the rows in the puzzle above? Circle or highlight them.

PUZZLE #2: CLASSICAL COMPOSERS

Fill in the blanks to form the last name of a composer in each row, reading across. The name must include the letter that you put in the highlighted column. Use each letter of the alphabet once to complete the puzzle. (No J, Q, or X.)

COMPOSER

A B C D E F G H I K L M N O P R S T U V W Y Z

#							(■)						
1	F	L	A	T	B	A		H	O	R	U	S	A
2	D	E	B	U	S	S		A	C	C	E	N	T
3	S	C	A	L	E	B		A	H	M	S	A	X
4	U	P	R	O	K	O		I	E	V	T	I	E
5	E	N	C	O	R	E		A	G	N	E	R	V
6	P	I	A	N	O	L		S	Z	T	U	B	A
7	A	M	E	N	D	E		S	S	O	H	N	Y
8	O	C	T	A	V	E		R	I	E	G	O	H
9	S	O	N	G	M	O		A	R	T	E	N	O
10	B	U	S	A	G	U		S	A	R	I	S	Y
11	C	O	D	A	M	A		I	N	O	T	R	O
12	M	A	R	C	A	O		I	N	O	T	E	S
13	B	E	A	T	B	R		B	R	E	R	T	O
14	S	L	O	P	E	L		V	R	L	U	T	E
15	S	C	U	H	C	H		O	V	S	K	Y	A
16	S	T	A	R	A	R		K	B	A	T	O	N
17	T	A	B	A	R	T		O	V	S	T	O	V
18	M	E	L	O	D	Y		I	C	H	O	O	Z
19	S	T	A	V	E	R		I	C	H	O	I	R
20	S	C	R	A	C	H		A	N	I	N	O	V
21	A	S	R	A	T	U		S	O	N	A	T	A
22	B	E	E	T	H	O		E	N	A	L	T	O
23	C	L	E	F	H	A		D	E	L	Y	R	E

NAME

FIRST NAME

	MATCH	CHOICE
A		Anton
B		Bela
C		Camille
D		Claude
E		Edvard
F		Felix
G		Franz
H		Frederic
I		George Frideric
J		Georges
K		Guiseppi
L		Gustav
M		Hector
N		Johann Sebastian
O		Johannes
P		Ludwig Van
Q		Maurice
R		Peter Ilyich
S		Richard
T		Richard
U		Serge
V		Sergei
W		Wolfgang Amadeus

Can you find 29 other musical words hidden across the rows in the puzzle? Circle or highlight them.   Now, match the first name of each composer.

PUZZLE #3: MUSICAL INSTRUMENTS

Fill in the blanks to form the name of a instrument in each row, reading across. The name must include the letter that you put in the highlighted column. Use each letter of the alphabet once to complete the puzzle. (No Q or W.)

Musical Instruments

	A	B	C	D	E	F	G	H	I	J	K	L	M	N	O	P	R	S	T	U	V	X	Y	Z
1	P	A	R	T	I	M			A	N	I	M	A	L										
2	S	O	U	S	A	P			O	N	E	N	E	T										
3	L	Y	R	E	B	A			S	O	N	U	S											
4	O	B	U	G	L	E			U	B	A	L	D	Y										
5	F	I	F	E	L	U			E	L	E	L	E	N										
6	C	L	A	R	I	N			T	V	I	B	E	S										
7	J	U	S	P	I	N			N	O	R	G	A	N										
8	C	O	R	N	E	T			I	O	L	I	N	Y										
9	F	S	N	A	R	E			R	U	M	A	D	S										
10	G	L	O	C	K	E			S	P	I	E	L	T										
11	M	O	H	A	R	P			C	C	O	L	O	R										
12	B	O	N	G	O	S			L	U	T	E	R	M										
13	T	A	N	A	X	Y			O	P	H	O	N	E										
14	H	A	F	R	E	N			H	H	O	R	N	R										
15	G	L	U	B	A	N			O	B	O	E	G	G										
16	A	V	I	O	L	A			I	T	H	E	R	T										
17	S	T	A	M	B	O			R	I	N	E	R	T										
18	F	A	C	E	L	L			C	H	I	M	E	S										
19	P	L	U	T	E	R			U	I	T	A	R	N										
20	B	E	L	L	S	A			O	P	H	O	N	E										
21	F	O	R	T	R	U			P	E	T	A	I	L										
22	G	O	N	G	Y	C			M	B	A	L	S	Y										
23	B	A	T	R	O	M			O	N	E	A	T	Z										
24	C	R	Y	C	M	A			A	C	A	S	C	H										

NAME

Fill in the first letter of the musical family for each instrument.

	FAMILY B/P/S/W	Musical Instruments
1		
2		
3		
...		

MUSICAL FAMILY

B	Brass
P	Percussion
S	Strings
W	Woodwinds

Can you find 14 other musical instruments hidden across the rows in the puzzle above? Circle or highlight them.

SECTION 1 - ALPHAGRAMS

PUZZLE #4: MUSICAL GENRES

Fill in the blanks to complete the name of a musical genre in each row across. The new word must include the letter that you put in the highlighted column.
Use each letter of the alphabet once to complete the puzzle. (No Q or X.)

NAME
_____

MUSICAL GENRE

A B C D E F G H I J K L M N O P R S T U V W Y Z

#														
1	P	S	A	L	M	O		A	T	O	R	I	O	_____
2	S	T	R	E	T	U		E	M	E	R	I	T	_____
3	R	A	M	A	R	C		V	E	R	B	A	L	_____
4	A	C	H	O	R	A		E	A	G	L	E	S	_____
5	C	A	P	R	E	L		D	E	B	A	T	E	_____
6	Y	O	U	R	H	A		S	O	D	Y	E	S	_____
7	I	S	E	R	E	N		D	E	L	U	G	E	_____
8	A	S	O	F	A	N		A	R	E	A	R	T	_____
9	B	U	S	T	M	O		E	T	R	Y	A	T	_____
10	M	U	S	I	C	S		M	P	H	O	N	Y	_____
11	U	N	D	O	F	U		U	E	S	T	E	R	_____
12	R	O	U	N	D	L		A	L	T	Z	O	O	_____
13	P	R	O	P	E	R		T	T	A	X	E	S	_____
14	R	E	A	D	I	M		N	U	E	T	O	N	_____
15	P	A	N	T	H	E		M	I	N	U	S	Y	_____
16	S	C	H	O	O	L		O	N	A	T	A	L	_____
17	H	Y	M	N	C	A		T	A	T	A	N	Y	_____
18	F	O	R	J	A	Z		O	C	T	E	T	O	_____
19	S	H	Y	M	N	O		L	U	E	S	K	Y	_____
20	Z	I	N	C	O	N		E	R	T	O	W	N	_____
21	T	O	U	C	A	N		C	T	U	R	N	E	_____
22	F	E	A	R	O	C		A	C	A	N	O	N	_____
23	N	A	V	A	H	O		I	V	E	A	C	H	_____
24	A	R	I	A	T	O		E	R	T	U	R	E	_____

Can you find these other musical genres hidden across the rows above?
Circle or highlight them: aria canon, hymn, octet, psalm, round.

PUZZLE #5: MUSICAL TERMS

Fill in the blanks to complete a musical term in each row, reading across. The new word must include the letter that you put in the highlighted column. Use each letter of the alphabet once to complete the puzzle. (No X.)

NAME _____

A B C D E F G H I J K L M N O P Q R S T U V W Y Z   **MUSICALS**

#							(highlight)						
1	L	O	C	O	N	C		R	T	S	I	N	G
2	W	I	N	T	E	R		A	L	F	L	A	T
3	A	R	C	O	N	D		C	T	O	R	A	L
4	I	S	T	A	F	F		U	A	R	T	E	T
5	T	R	Y	F	O	L		S	O	N	G	U	M
6	G	A	S	T	A	N		A	L	S	T	E	M
7	W	E	T	E	M	P		S	C	A	L	E	N
8	F	A	R	R	A	N		E	M	E	N	T	O
9	U	B	A	T	O	N		A	Z	Z	O	O	M
10	S	H	A	R	M	O		Y	T	R	I	L	L
11	A	C	U	T	R	H		T	H	M	A	T	H
12	F	O	R	C	O	M		O	S	E	R	U	N
13	S	H	A	R	P	C		O	R	D	R	U	M
14	B	A	D	Y	N	A		I	C	S	T	A	R
15	S	T	I	E	M	E		S	U	R	E	A	L
16	I	N	A	C	C	I		E	N	T	A	L	Y
17	A	R	M	F	U	N		S	O	N	C	U	E
18	V	E	R	S	E	T		I	P	L	E	T	Y
19	B	E	A	T	V	I		R	A	T	O	N	E
20	R	E	S	T	M	E		O	D	Y	A	R	D
21	P	O	R	C	H	E		T	R	A	N	G	E
22	N	A	C	C	L	E		E	N	C	O	R	E
23	M	E	T	E	R	A		C	E	N	T	E	D
24	N	O	T	E	O	C		A	V	E	R	A	G
25	S	A	W	O	O	D		I	N	D	S	U	M

Now can you find 20 other musical term hidden across the rows in the finished puzzle above? Circle or highlight them.

PUZZLE #6: ITALIAN MUSICAL TERMS

Fill in the blanks to form an Italian musical term in each row, reading across. The word must include the letter that you put in the highlighted column. Use each letter of the alphabet once to complete the puzzle. (No B, H, J, K, W, X, or Y.)

#	A	C	D	E	F	G	I	L	M	N	O	P	Q	R	S	T	U	V	Z
1	S	I	N	E	O	F		O	R	T	E	S	T						
2	T	R	E	S	P	R		S	S	I	V	O	W						
3	C	O	F	F	E	R		A	T	A	B	L	E						
4	P	U	P	A	N	N		S	S	I	M	O	T						
5	A	Z	S	F	O	R		A	N	D	O	O	R						
6	M	A	R	C	A	T		M	U	L	T	O	N						
7	M	A	C	R	E	S		E	N	D	O	W	N						
8	W	H	A	L	E	G		T	O	F	I	S	H						
9	A	R	R	I	V	I		A	C	E	L	L	O						
10	U	D	I	M	N	N		E	N	D	O	L	L						
11	C	A	T	L	A	R		O	A	P	L	U	S						
12	P	R	T	A	R	R		A	N	D	O	R	N						
13	N	O	R	M	A	E		T	O	S	O	N	G						
14	A	M	A	T	H	A		D	A	N	T	E	N						
15	A	C	C	E	L	E		A	N	D	O	R	Y						
16	A	C	T	R	N	E		U	I	L	O	W							
17	S	T	A	N	D	O		C	E	L	E	R	Y						
18	S	T	A	C	C	A		O	T	T	E	R	N						
19	D	I	V	I	D	E		R	E	S	T	O	N						

NAME _____

Italian Term _____ | **DEFINITION MATCH** _____

DEFINITION CHOICES

A	Emphasized, accented
B	Slow tempo
C	Hold; pause
D	Lively
E	Very fast
F	Majestically
G	Loud
H	Sudden strong accent
I	Gradually louder
J	Detached sounds
K	Walking tempo
L	Smooth, connected
M	Expressively
N	Gradually softer
O	Quietly; calmly
P	Gradually slower
Q	Very soft
R	Sweetly
S	Gradually faster

Now, match the term with its definition.

HELPFUL WORD LISTS

BROADWAY MUSICAL WORD LIST	CLASSICAL COMPOSERS WORD LIST	INSTRUMENTS WORD LIST	MUSICAL TERMS WORD LIST
ACT	ACCENT	BELLS	BATON
ACTORS	ALTO	BONGOS	BEAT
BOWS	BATON	BUGLE	CUE
CAN CAN	CHOIR	CHIMES	CUT
CREW	CHORUS	CORNET	DRUM
CUE	CLEF	FIFE	ENCORE
DANCE	CODA	GONG	FLAT
FLY	CUE	HARP	METER
HAIR	ENCORE	LUTE	NOTE
I DO, I DO	FLAT	LYRE	RANGE
LIVE	JAZZ	OBOE	REST
MAKE UP	LUTE	ORGAN	SCALE
PIPPIN	LYRE	VIBES	SHARP
PIT	MARCH	VIOLA	SING
RENT	MELODY		STAFF
SCORE	NOTES		STEM
SCRIPT	OCTAVE		TIE
SET	OPERA		TONE
STAGE	PIANO		TRILL
	REST		VERSE
	SAX		
	SCALE		
	SONATA		
	SONG		
	STAVE		
	TIE		
	TREBLE		
	TRIO		
	TUBA		

SECTION 2
MATCHING PUZZLES

PUZZLE #7: COMPOSERS

Match the composer with the composition.
Write the correct letter in the answer column
next to the composer's name.

NAME _____

	COMPOSER	ANSWER		COMPOSITION
1	Georges Bizet	_____	A	Clair de Lune, La Mer
2	George Frideric Handel	_____	B	Eine Kleine Nachtmusik, Don Giovanni
3	Ludwig van Beethoven	_____	C	The Four Seasons
4	Peter Ilyich Tchaikovsky	_____	D	New World Symphony
5	Claude Debussy	_____	E	The Planets
6	Johann Sebastian Bach	_____	F	Aida
7	Maurice Ravel	_____	G	Surprise Symphony
8	Johannes Brahms	_____	H	Finlandia
9	Gustav Holst	_____	I	Carmen
10	Antonin Dvořák	_____	J	Brandenburg Concertos, B-Minor Mass
11	Giuseppi Verdi	_____	K	1812 Overture, The Nutcracker
12	Jean Sibelius	_____	L	Messiah, Water Music
13	Wolfgang Amadeus Mozart	_____	M	German Requiem, Liebeslieder Waltzes
14	Franz Joseph Haydn	_____	N	Bolero
15	Antonio Vivaldi	_____	O	Für Elise, Moonlight Sonata

PUZZLE #8: CONTEMPORARY BROADWAY

_____

NAME

Match the song title with the Broadway musical it came from. Every musical will be used one or more times. Write the letter of the musical in the answer column next to the song title.

	SONG TITLE	ANSWER		BROADWAY MUSICAL
1	Magic To Do	_____	A	A Chorus Line
2	Dancing Through Life	_____	C	Mamma Mia
3	The Circle of Life	_____	E	Grease
4	One	_____	G	Cats
5	You Can't Stop the Beat	_____	H	Pippin
6	Greased Lightnin'	_____	I	Rent
7	Popular	_____	N	Beauty and the Beast
8	Be Our Guest	_____	O	The Lion King
9	Memory	_____	R	Wicked
10	Hakuna Matata	_____	S	Phantom of the Opera
11	The Music of the Night	_____	T	Hairspray
12	Good Morning Baltimore	_____		
13	For Good	_____		
14	What I Did For Love	_____		
15	Welcome to the 60's	_____		
16	Seasons of Love	_____		
17	We Go Together	_____		
18	The Winner Takes It All	_____		

Now write the letter of the answer for each numbered song title on the blanks below to find something needed for a good musical show.

___ ___ ___ ___ ___   ___ ___ ___ ___ ___ ___ ___ ___ ___ ___ ___ ___ ___
9 13 17 4 12   10 7 18 1 6 11 15 2 14 5 16 3 8

PUZZLE #9: CLASSIC BROADWAY

Match the song title with the Broadway musical it came from. Every musical will be used one or more times. Write the letter of the musical in the answer column next to the song title.

	SONG TITLE	ANSWER		BROADWAY MUSICAL
1	Tonight	_____	A	The Sound of Music
2	I Could Have Danced All Night	_____	B	Porgy and Bess
3	My Favorite Things	_____	C	South Pacific
4	Tomorrow	_____	D	George M
5	Food, Glorious Food	_____	E	Guys and Dolls
6	People	_____	I	The King and I
7	Some Enchanted Evening	_____	K	Oklahoma
8	If I Were a Rich Man	_____	L	The Man of La Mancha
9	Somewhere	_____	M	The Music Man
10	Do-Re-Mi	_____	N	Annie
11	Summertime	_____	O	Oliver
12	The Impossible Dream	_____	R	Fiddler on the Roof
13	On the Street Where You Live	_____	S	Showboat
14	Getting to Know You	_____	U	Funny Girl
15	Tradition	_____	W	West Side Story
16	Climb Every Mountain	_____	Y	My Fair Lady
17	Consider Yourself	_____		
18	Ol' Man River	_____		
19	Seventy-Six Trombones	_____		
20	Oh, What a Beautiful Morning	_____		
21	Luck Be a Lady	_____		
22	I'm a Yankee Doodle Dandy	_____		

Now write the letter of the answer for each numbered song title on the blanks below to find the theme for this puzzle.

___ ___ ___　　___ ___ ___ ___　　___ ___ ___ ___ ___ ___ ___ ___　　___ ___ ___ ___ ___ ___ ___ ___
4 21 9　　2 17 8 20　　11 15 5 10 22 1 16 13　　19 6 18 14 7 3 12

SECTION 3
NAME THAT TUNE

PUZZLE #10: CHRISTMAS CAROLS

Here are ten well-known Christmas Carols. Match the titles with the melodies.

NAME

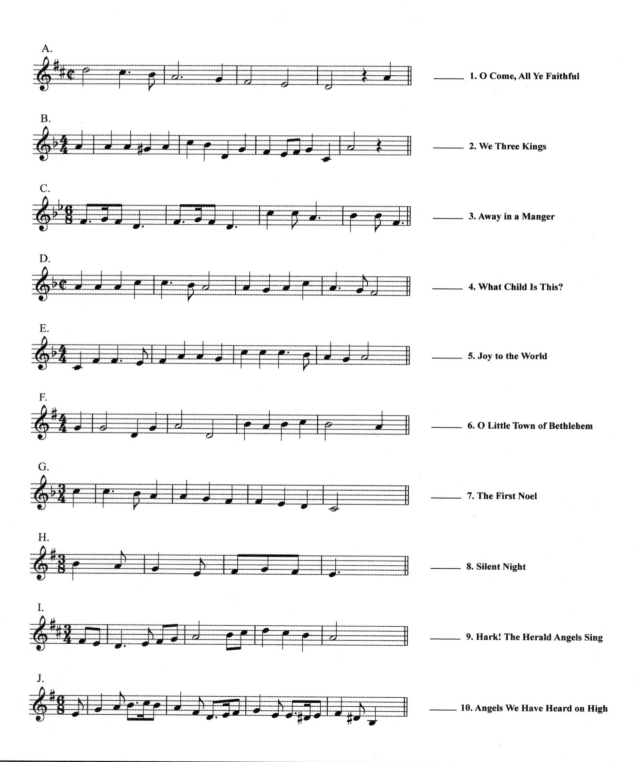

——— 1. O Come, All Ye Faithful

——— 2. We Three Kings

——— 3. Away in a Manger

——— 4. What Child Is This?

——— 5. Joy to the World

——— 6. O Little Town of Bethlehem

——— 7. The First Noel

——— 8. Silent Night

——— 9. Hark! The Herald Angels Sing

——— 10. Angels We Have Heard on High

PUZZLE #11: CHRISTMAS SONGS

Here are ten well-known Christmas songs. Match
the titles with the melodies.

NAME

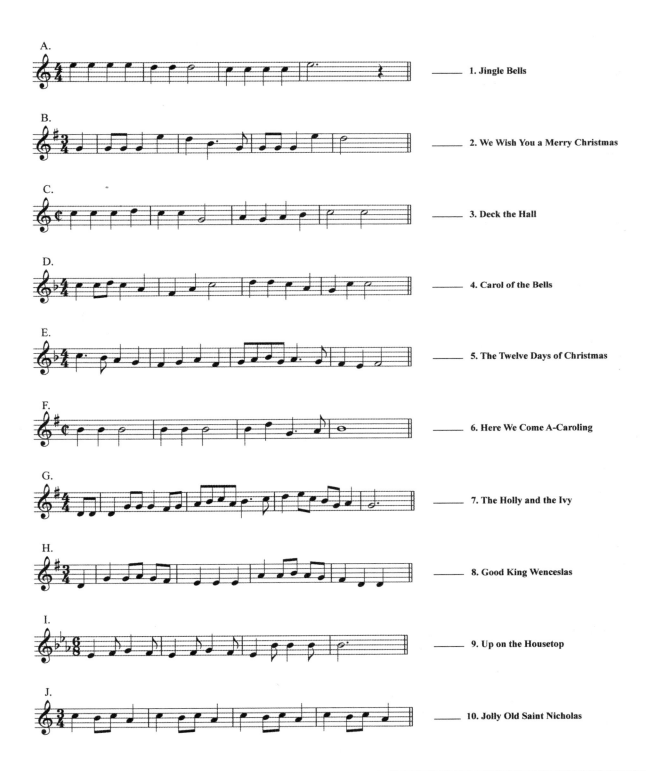

_____ 1. Jingle Bells

_____ 2. We Wish You a Merry Christmas

_____ 3. Deck the Hall

_____ 4. Carol of the Bells

_____ 5. The Twelve Days of Christmas

_____ 6. Here We Come A-Caroling

_____ 7. The Holly and the Ivy

_____ 8. Good King Wenceslas

_____ 9. Up on the Housetop

_____ 10. Jolly Old Saint Nicholas

PUZZLE #12:   CHILDHOOD SONGS

Here are ten well-known childhood songs. Match the titles with the melodies.

NAME

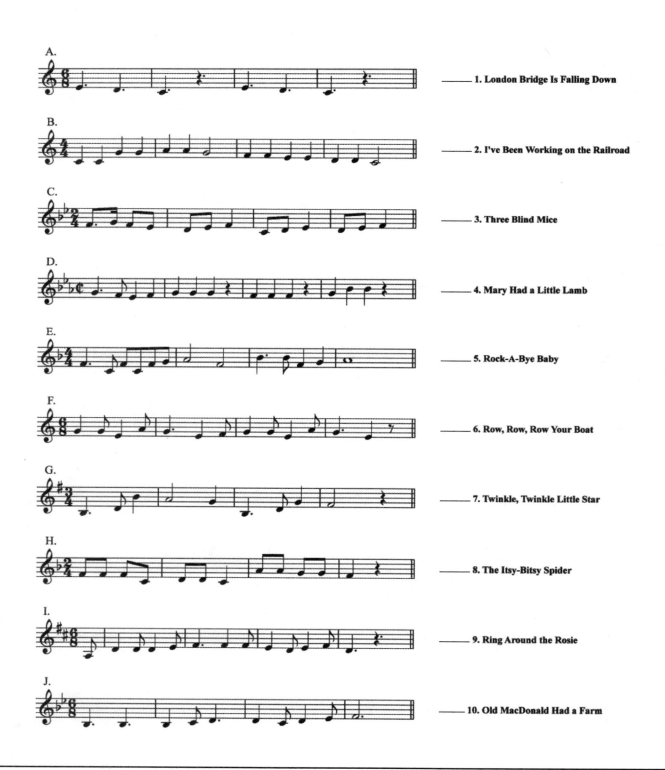

———— **1. London Bridge Is Falling Down**

———— **2. I've Been Working on the Railroad**

———— **3. Three Blind Mice**

———— **4. Mary Had a Little Lamb**

———— **5. Rock-A-Bye Baby**

———— **6. Row, Row, Row Your Boat**

———— **7. Twinkle, Twinkle Little Star**

———— **8. The Itsy-Bitsy Spider**

———— **9. Ring Around the Rosie**

———— **10. Old MacDonald Had a Farm**

PUZZLE #13: CAMP SONGS

Here are ten well-known camp songs. Match the titles with the melodies.

NAME

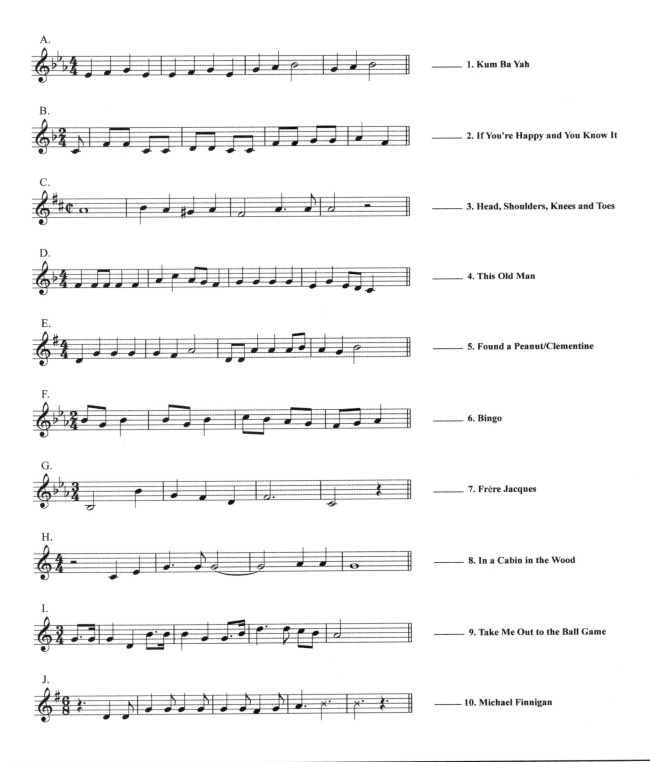

_____ 1. Kum Ba Yah

_____ 2. If You're Happy and You Know It

_____ 3. Head, Shoulders, Knees and Toes

_____ 4. This Old Man

_____ 5. Found a Peanut/Clementine

_____ 6. Bingo

_____ 7. Frère Jacques

_____ 8. In a Cabin in the Wood

_____ 9. Take Me Out to the Ball Game

_____ 10. Michael Finnigan

SECTION 4
MUSICAL SUDOKU

PUZZLE #14-17: MUSIC NOTE

Complete the grid so each row, column, and 3-by-3 box (in bold borders) contains every letter of the puzzle. The puzzles get progressively harder on this page.

NAME _____

14. MUSIC NOTE

U		I			M			T
	C			I	E	M		O
T			U		S	C		
	I	U	M	O			E	
M	O						S	U
	N			E	U	I	O	
		M	E		T			N
O		C	N	M			T	
E			C			U		I

15. MUSIC NOTE

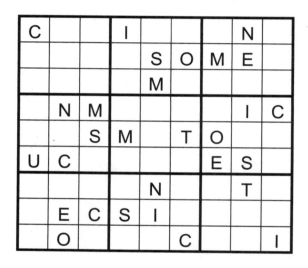

C			I				N	
				S	O	M	E	
			M					
	N	M					I	C
		S	M		T	O		
U	C					E	S	
				N			T	
	E	C	S	I				
	O				C			I

16. MUSIC NOTE

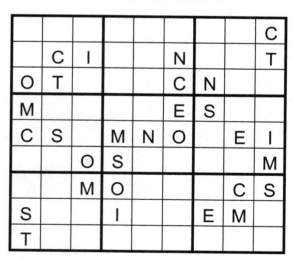

								C
	C	I			N			T
O	T				C	N		
M				E	S			
C	S		M	N	O		E	I
		O	S					M
		M	O				C	S
S			I			E	M	
T								

17. MUSIC NOTE

	O	T	S			C	N	
						S		T
M			T		N			
	S				T	O		
		C				I		
		I	O				E	
		N		C				E
T		N						
	E	M			O	U	C	

PUZZLE #18-21: TRIANGLES

Complete the grid so each row, column, and 3-by-3 box (in bold borders) contains every letter of the puzzle. The puzzles get progressively harder on this page.

NAME _____

18. TRIANGLES

		G			R			
I	N			E			G	A
A			I	N		T		L
L	G	N			S		T	
	E					R		
	T		G			S	I	N
E		R		G	T			S
N	S			R			A	T
			L			I		

19. TRIANGLES

S		A		N				
					T		L	E
	L		G		I			
A		T						L
	E	L		G		I		
I						N		R
		N		A		E		
N	E		I					
			G			T		N

20. TRIANGLES

	E	A		N		R		
G			T		I	L		E
		L			A			
T		R				I		
		L				G		N
		T		G				
A		G	S		N			T
		S			E		N	G

21. TRIANGLES

		S				I		
I			A					
E				I		N	L	S
L							I	N
N			R		L			G
A	T							R
G	N	I		A				L
				G				E
	E					R		

PUZZLE #22-25:   C MAJOR KEY

Complete the grid so each row, column, and 3-by-3 box (in bold borders) contains every letter of the puzzle. The puzzles get progressively harder on this page.

_____

NAME

22. C MAJOR KEY

			C			J	O	R
A	E				O			M
		O		Y	R		K	
J				O		Y	C	
K			Y		M			J
	R	E		C				O
	Y		J	M		R		
R				E			A	C
E	C	K			A			

23. C MAJOR KEY

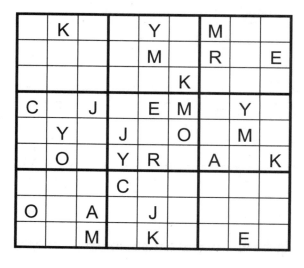

	K			Y		M		
		M			R		E	
					K			
C		J		E	M		Y	
	Y		J		O		M	
	O		Y	R		A		K
		C						
O		A		J				
	M		K			E		

24. C MAJOR KEY

C	Y				K			R
R	O				M			
		M	R					
		J			O	K		A
Y			K		A			M
E		K	C			O		
					Y	C		
			E				R	K
O				A			M	Y

25. C MAJOR KEY

		K			Y	O	J	
			C				K	A
	C				J			
A	E					K		J
			J		E			
M		O					Y	E
			R				E	
J	Y			A				
	K	M	Y			R		

PUZZLE #26-29: A MINOR KEY

Complete the grid so each row, column, and 3-by-3 box (in bold borders) contains every letter of the puzzle. The puzzles get progressively harder on this page.

NAME _____

26. A MINOR KEY

O	R	Y	N					
M				O	N		Y	
		A		E	I		M	
I			K		Y	A		
R			E		A			I
	O	M		Y				K
	K		M	A		R		
N			O	K				E
					Y	K	I	M

27. A MINOR KEY

M			K	N				Y
			A		M			
O		E				A		M
		K	E		O	N		
I				M				A
		A	I		R	E		
E		M				R		N
		M		E				
A			R	Y				I

28. A MINOR KEY

	A			I		O		
R						Y		
	O			Y	E		K	
		O			N	E	Y	
		A			K			
K	E	M				O		
O		I	A			K		
	Y							E
	K		I			A		

29. A MINOR KEY

K		Y	A					
	E				M			
	A	I			R		N	
				I		A	Y	E
N								I
E	I	R			A			
	R			E		K	A	
				N			O	
					Y	N		R

PUZZLE #30-33: SIGNATURE

Complete the grid so each row, column, and 3-by-3 box (in bold borders) contains every letter of the puzzle. The puzzles get progressively harder on this page.

NAME _____

30. SIGNATURE

N	I		A	E				
R		S		I			T	
A		G				U	E	
		R	I					E
	G	I	U		S	R	N	
T				G		A		
	U	E						N
	N			S		I		R
			U	A		G	S	

31. SIGNATURE

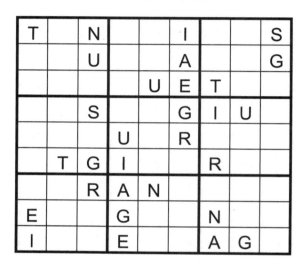

T		N			I			S
		U			A			G
			U	E	T			
	S			G	I	U		
		U		R				
	T	G	I			R		
	R	A	N					
E			G			N		
I			E			A	G	

32. SIGNATURE

		T	U			S		
	R			N				
S			G			R	E	U
	G		R		A			
E								S
		U		T		I		
T	N	S		G			R	
			S			G		
		G		U	N			

33. SIGNATURE

	E		S		U		A	
	R		N		G		E	
A								G
		G	A	R	S			
T								R
		E	G	S	A			
S								E
	U		I	A			N	
	T		R	E			S	

PUZZLE #34-37: INTERVALS

Complete the grid so each row, column, and 3-by-3 box (in bold borders) contains every letter of the puzzle. The puzzles get progressively harder on this page.

NAME _____

34. INTERVALS

		I	R	L				T
	S	A	I			L		
	E			V	A			R
			A	R	S	N	V	
		T				I		
S	A	N	V	E				
I		R	E				A	
	N				T	L	V	
E			L	S		N		

35. INTERVALS

E	S			I		L		V
L		N		V				
	V		R					
				A		L		
T	R						I	S
	I		E					
					I		N	
			R			V		A
S			E	V	A		R	L

36. INTERVALS

			I		N			
V		N	L					
	S	E						
S			A				T	L
	N	A	V		L	I	R	
R	L			T				S
					N	V		
					V	L		A
		T		E				

37. INTERVALS

	N		R		E		V	
				I				
T	E						A	I
		E	L		R	V		
		R	N		S	I		
V	A						T	E
			L					
		L		I	V		S	

PUZZLE #38-41:   CLARINETS

Complete the grid so each row, column, and 3-by-3 box (in bold borders) contains every letter of the puzzle. The puzzles get progressively harder on this page.

_____

NAME

38. CLARINETS

E		A					L	N
	R	I	A	L				
T		S		R		C		
		C		E				A
R	E		N		T		I	S
S			R			L		
	I			T		S		R
			N	A	T	E		
L	N					I		C

39. CLARINETS

	I	S	R					
						S		N
A			S	E		T		
		R	E		S			C
C								L
S			A		R	N		
		L		R	N			A
I		A						
						E	C	L

40. CLARINETS

	C		T	N		A		
		C			N			S
E	T			S				I
					R	I	N	
		T			A			
L	R	E						
A			R			E	T	
T		R		C				
		L	T	S		R		

41. CLARINETS

		S			I	R		
	T		N					
	A			E				T
A	L		I	R	E			
N								A
			A	N	S		C	I
C				T			L	
				A			N	
	E	R			S			

PUZZLE #42-45: BARITONES

Complete the grid so each row, column, and 3-by-3 box (in bold borders) contains every letter of the puzzle. The puzzles get progressively harder on this page.

NAME _____

42. BARITONES

	B	R		E	N			
T		N					E	S
O		I		B			A	
I				B	E			
B	T		O		S		R	I
		A		T				N
	R			O		I		B
E	S					R		A
			N	S		O	T	

43. BARITONES

			B	R	T			S
N	T					O		
	A	O	N			B		
S				R				
		E					I	
			S					A
		A			I	N	R	
	E						A	O
O			A		B	S		

44. BARITONES

A		N	R	B				
T				A	N	E		
	R		T					B
	E		B		I	T		N
I								A
S		A	E		N		I	
N				R		B		
	A	R	N					E
				I	B	R		T

45. BARITONES

					T		E	O
	N		A			S		B
B				I	A			R
	T							
S	I			A			B	T
							A	
E		O	B					A
T			A		O		I	
I	S		T					

33

PUZZLE #46-49: DYNAMICS

Complete the grid so each row, column, and 3-by-3 box (in bold borders) contains every item in the puzzle key. The puzzles get progressively harder on this page.

Puzzle Key: pp, p, mp, mf, f, ff, sfz, $<$, $>$

NAME _____

46. DYNAMICS

	sfz	p		>	<	ff		
f		ff		pp		<		>
			mf				f	
<	mp	>			f			sfz
mf								pp
sfz			mp			p	>	f
	<			p				
ff		sfz		mf			>	mp
		mp	sfz	f		pp	mf	

47. DYNAMICS

	mf					ff		mp
ff			p					<
	>		mf	ff	mp		sfz	
				<	p			
		sfz				mp	pp	
			f	pp				
	sfz		>	mf	pp		<	
<					ff			>
>		mf					p	

48. DYNAMICS

	f	<			sfz			
		mp		mf				<
pp			<	mp		ff		mf
		f						
		p	sfz		f	>		
						p		
sfz		pp		ff	<			p
mp				f		pp		
			p			mf	ff	

49. DYNAMICS

	f		pp					
ff				<		mf		pp
		ff				mp	sfz	
		sfz			>	p		
	ff	<				pp	f	
		pp	p			mp		
mp	p				ff			
sfz			mf		p			mp
			>			p		

PUZZLE #50-53: MUSICAL SCALE

Complete the grid so each row, column, and 3-by-3 box (in bold borders) contains every item in the puzzle key. The puzzles get progressively harder on this page.

Puzzle Key: C, D, E, F, G, A, B, ♯, ♭

NAME _____

50. MUSICAL SCALE

	B			F		E		A
		G	D		♭	F		
♯	D				G			C
G				C	B			
E	♭		♯		A		C	F
		D	F					E
B		♭				♯		D
	C	A		♯	G			
F		E		A		♭		

51. MUSICAL SCALE

C	B		F					
A			B	D				
	F						B	D
G				C	A		F	
		F				E		
	E		G	♯				A
F	C					A		
			♭	E				F
			♯			D	E	

52. MUSICAL SCALE

	E			♭	F		A	
F								
			B	E		G	♯	
♭		C		G		E		
			F		♭			
		G		♯		B		F
E	A		♭	F				
								D
	♭		C	D		B		

53. MUSICAL SCALE

A	♯			C				
			A			♭		♯
		♭					D	G
♭			F		G	B		
		B				♯		
		♯	♭		B			D
B	E					D		
D		A			♯			
							B	E

PUZZLE #54-57: MUSICAL SYMBOLS

Complete the grid so each row, column, and 3-by-3 box (in bold borders) contains every item in the puzzle key. The puzzles get progressively harder on this page.

Puzzle Key: ♯, ♭, ♪, ♩, 𝅗𝅥, 𝅝, 𝄞, 𝄢, 𝄽

NAME _____

54. MUSICAL SYMBOLS

55. MUSICAL SYMBOLS

56. MUSICAL SYMBOLS

57. MUSICAL SYMBOLS

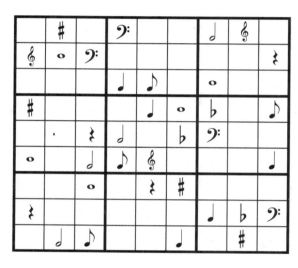

SECTION 5
CROSSWORDS

PUZZLE #58:   TREBLE CLEF CROSSWORD 1

Identify the correct letter name of each treble clef note, then write the word in the appropriate place on the puzzle.

NAME

DOWN

ACROSS

PUZZLE #59: TREBLE CLEF CROSSWORD 2

Identify the correct letter name of each treble clef note, then write the word in the appropriate place on the puzzle.

NAME _____

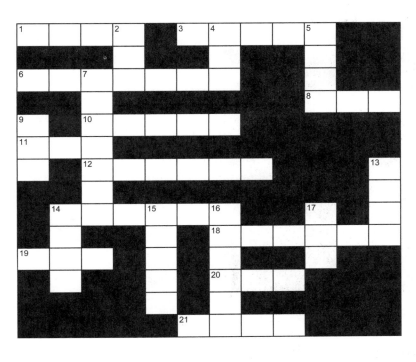

DOWN

ACROSS

PUZZLE #60:   BASS CLEF CROSSWORD 1

Identify the correct letter name of each bass clef note, then write the word in the appropriate place on the puzzle.

NAME

DOWN

ACROSS

PUZZLE #61: BASS CLEF CROSSWORD 2

Identify the correct letter name of each bass clef note, then write the word in the appropriate place on the puzzle.

NAME _____

DOWN

ACROSS

PUZZLE #62: CONTEMPORARY BROADWAY

Complete the title of the Broadway musicals by filling in the blank. For clues without the blank, fill in the theatre term that is described.

NAME _____

ACROSS

- 2 Mary _____
- 5 Moving rhythmically to music
- 7 _____ Todd
- 10 Items handled by actors during a show
- 11 _____ Rotten Scoundrels
- 12 The Color _____
- 14 _____ and the Beast
- 16 A Little _____ Music
- 19 The _____ King
- 21 A musical performance by two people
- 22 The theatre part where the actor performs
- 23 _____ Boys
- 24 The cast, crew, and others involved in a show; also the name of a Sondheim musical

DOWN

- 1 Words spoken by the actors
- 3 The music which begins a performance
- 4 High _____ Musical
- 5 The _____ Chaperone
- 6 A humorous play
- 8 The scenery and furniture that create a scene
- 9 _____ and Hyde
- 10 The _____ of the Opera
- 13 A _____ Line
- 14 Legally _____
- 15 Male performers in a play
- 17 The Secret _____
- 18 Thoroughly _____ Millie
- 20 _____ Mia

PUZZLE #63: CLASSIC BROADWAY

Complete the title of the Broadway musicals by filling in the blank. For clues without the blank, fill in the theatre term that is described.

NAME

ACROSS

3 The Man of La _____
5 South _____
8 The written form of a musical composition
9 Guys and _____
13 _____ Goes
14 The people who do work backstage
16 The _____ and I
17 The words to a song
20 Annie Get Your _____
22 The painted backdrop on a stage
24 The sunken area where the orchestra sits
25 _____, Dolly
26 The _____ Game
29 _____ Charity
30 Funny _____
31 A female performer in a play
32 Lift or raise a set piece or lights
33 An actors first appearance in a show
34 Movement to music

DOWN

1 The lines spoken by the cast
2 Bye, Bye, _____
4 The drapery that hides the stage
6 The _____ Man
7 The clothing worn by an actor in a show
10 What the actors do in a curtain call
11 _____ on the Roof
12 The cosmetics used on the face
15 My _____ Lady
18 42nd _____
19 The actors chosen for a show
21 The printed text of the show
23 Kiss Me, _____
24 _____ and Bess
27 A section of stage that goes into the audience
28 A passageway through the seating area
29 West _____ Story

SECTION 6
CRYPTO-LISTS

PUZZLE #64: BROADWAY MUSICALS

Crypto-lists are lists of related words and phrases that have been translated into a code. The code is the same for every word in the list. For example, if G represents A in one word, it will represent A in every word on the list. Your job is to find the right code so that every word fits the theme of this puzzle.

NAME

_____

HINT: Start thinking of answers that might fit the theme and try out that code. Or you can start by looking for common words that have the same letter pattern. Not every letter of the alphabet will be used in the puzzle.

ORIGINAL LETTER REPRESENTS

A	B	C	D	E	F	G	H	I	J	K	L	M

N	O	P	Q	R	S	T	U	V	W	X	Y	Z

1. Z H E M

2. T D N E H

3. E C T ▓ M A F X B ▓ A G ▓ U F M N Z

4. U Q ▓ G H N S ▓ J H B Q

5. E C T ▓ Y N X R ▓ H X B ▓ N

6. I N Z Y T B

7. R F Q M ▓ H X B ▓ B A J J M

8. C H N S M K S H Q

9. U H U U H ▓ U N H

10. H X X N T

11. H ▓ Z C A S F M ▓ J N X T

12. E C T ▓ U F M N Z ▓ U H X

PUZZLE #65: CHRISTMAS SONGS

NAME ______________________________

Crypto-lists are lists of related words and phrases that have been translated into a code. The code is the same for every word in the list. For example, if G represents A in one word, it will represent A in every word on the list. Your job is to find the right code so that every word fits the theme of this puzzle.

HINT: Start thinking of answers that might fit the theme and try out that code. Or you can start by looking for common words that have the same letter pattern. Not every letter of the alphabet will be used in the puzzle.

ORIGINAL LETTER REPRESENTS

A	B	C	D	E	F	G	H	I	J	K	L	M

N	O	P	Q	R	S	T	U	V	W	X	Y	Z

1. R J U Q F Z   K F U U R
2. V F Z F   B C H F R   R X G M X   B U X E R
3. E O   C G   M V F   V C E R F M C O
4. A F B I   M V F   V X U U
5. W J G D U F   K F U U R
6. U F M   J M   R G C L
7. L V J M F   B V Z J R M H X R
8. R U F J D V   Z J A F
9. S Z C R M P   M V F   R G C L H X G

PUZZLE #66:   CHRISTMAS CAROLS

Crypto-lists are lists of related words and phrases that have been translated into a code. The code is the same for every word in the list. For example, if G represents A in one word, it will represent A in every word on the list. Your job is to find the right code so that every word fits the theme of this puzzle.

NAME _____

HINT: Start thinking of answers that might fit the theme and try out that code. Or you can start by looking for common words that have the same letter pattern. Not every letter of the alphabet will be used in the puzzle.

ORIGINAL LETTER REPRESENTS

A	B	C	D	E	F	G	H	I	J	K	L	M

N	O	P	Q	R	S	T	U	V	W	X	Y	Z

1. Q X Q F ▨ U E ▨ Q ▨ Y Q E T K H

2. O N K ▨ G U H C O ▨ E S K R

3. X N Q O ▨ W N U R J ▨ U C ▨ O N U C

4. S ▨ N S R F ▨ E U T N O

5. B S F ▨ O S ▨ O N K ▨ X S H R J

6. X K ▨ O N H K K ▨ P U E T C

7. R U O O R K ▨ J H A Y Y K H ▨ I S F

8. S ▨ W S Y K ▨ Q R R ▨ F K ▨ G Q U O N G A R

9. C U R K E O ▨ E U T N O

PUZZLE #67: CLASSICAL COMPOSERS

Crypto-lists are lists of related words and phrases that have been translated into a code. The code is the same for every word in the list. For example, if G represents A in one word, it will represent A in every word on the list. Your job is to find the right code so that every word fits the theme of this puzzle.

NAME

_____

HINT: Start thinking of answers that might fit the theme and try out that code. Or you can start by looking for common words that have the same letter pattern. Not every letter of the alphabet will be used in the puzzle.

ORIGINAL LETTER REPRESENTS

A	B	C	D	E	F	G	H	I	J	K	L	M

N	O	P	Q	R	S	T	U	V	W	X	Y	Z

1. C J F R X X ▨ T Z Q R T V H R X ▨ Q R E F

2. G O Z N Z O H E ▨ E F J L H X

3. M Z J O M Z ▨ G O H N Z O H E ▨ F R X N Z D

4. M P T V R I ▨ U R F D Z O

5. D P N S H M ▨ I R X ▨ Q Z Z V F J I Z X

6. G O R X W ▨ D H T W V

7. E D R P N Z ▨ N Z Q P T T K

8. U R P O H E Z ▨ O R I Z D

9. R X V J X H J ▨ I H I R D N H

10. C J F R X X Z T ▨ Q O R F U T

49

PUZZLE #68: MODERN COMPOSERS

Crypto-lists are lists of related words and phrases that have been translated into a code. The code is the same for every word in the list. For example, if G represents A in one word, it will represent A in every word on the list. Your job is to find the right code so that every word fits the theme of this puzzle.

NAME

HINT: Start thinking of answers that might fit the theme and try out that code. Or you can start by looking for common words that have the same letter pattern. Not every letter of the alphabet will be used in the puzzle.

ORIGINAL LETTER REPRESENTS

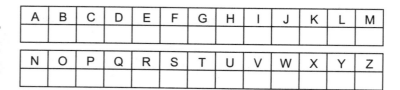

A	B	C	D	E	F	G	H	I	J	K	L	M

N	O	P	Q	R	S	T	U	V	W	X	Y	Z

1. N F E B T R ▓ O O P D E ▓ R T I I T B

2. J P O T ▓ X P B G T B

3. O T B P D ▓ N F E T B A P F

4. T O G P F ▓ W P K F

5. U T P B U T ▓ U T B A K R C F

6. N N B P F ▓ J P X O N F E

7. K T F B D ▓ L N F J C F C

8. W P K F ▓ R C O O C N L A

9. O T P F N B E ▓ I T B F A G T C F

10. W P K F ▓ X K C O O C X ▓ A P Q A N

PUZZLE #69: MUSICAL INSTRUMENTS

Crypto-lists are lists of related words and phrases that
have been translated into a code. The code is the same for
every word in the list. For example, if G represents A in one
word, it will represent A in every word on the list. Your job
is to find the right code so that every word fits the theme of
this puzzle.

NAME

*HINT: Start thinking of answers that might fit the theme
and try out that code. Or you can start by looking for
common words that have the same letter pattern. Not
every letter of the alphabet will be used in the puzzle.*

**ORIGINAL
LETTER
REPRESENTS**

A	B	C	D	E	F	G	H	I	J	K	L	M

N	O	P	Q	R	S	T	U	V	W	X	Y	Z

1 | C | Q | L | W | K |

2 | O | U | G | X | D |

3 | K | H | K | D |

4 | R | L | Y | K | C | M | K | W | D |

5 | X | J | G | T | C | D | X |

6 | E | U | L | J | Q | W | D | X |

7 | V | J | G | T | R |

8 | O | J | D | W | E | M | ▓ | M | K | J | W |

9 | N | Q | K | U | Q | W |

10 | E | D | U | U | K |

11 | X | G | H | L |

12 | X | J | K | T | H | K | W | D |

PUZZLE #70: SONGS BY THE BEATLES

Crypto-lists are lists of related words and phrases that have been translated into a code. The code is the same for every word in the list. For example, if G represents A in one word, it will represent A in every word on the list. Your job is to find the right code so that every word fits the theme of this puzzle.

NAME

HINT: Start thinking of answers that might fit the theme and try out that code. Or you can start by looking for common words that have the same letter pattern. Not every letter of the alphabet will be used in the puzzle.

ORIGINAL
LETTER
REPRESENTS

A	B	C	D	E	F	G	H	I	J	K	L	M

N	O	P	Q	R	S	T	U	V	W	X	Y	Z

1. H Y C ▮ U N A C H ▮ W N M

2. S Q B F C S ▮ S N ▮ T Q G C

3. Y C U Z

4. W C U U N L ▮ H M D K V T Q J C

5. W C H S C T G V W

6. Y C W ▮ X M G C

7. Z V Z C T D V B F ▮ L T Q S C T

8. V ▮ Y V T G ▮ G V W H ▮ J Q R Y S

9. R C S ▮ D V B F

PUZZLE #71:   FAVORITE KIDS' SONGS

Crypto-lists are lists of related words and phrases that have been translated into a code. The code is the same for every word in the list. For example, if G represents A in one word, it will represent A in every word on the list. Your job is to find the right code so that every word fits the theme of this puzzle.

NAME

HINT: Start thinking of answers that might fit the theme and try out that code. Or you can start by looking for common words that have the same letter pattern. Not every letter of the alphabet will be used in the puzzle.

ORIGINAL LETTER REPRESENTS

A	B	C	D	E	F	G	H	I	J	K	L	M

N	O	P	Q	R	S	T	U	V	W	X	Y	Z

1. L N Y   M D T Z Y T   S J   L N Y   W Y P P

2. L N T Y Y   U P S J W   Z S E Y

3. Z D T K   N D W   D   P S L L P Y   P D Z U

4. I F I   V F Y A   L N Y   O Y D A Y P

5. T F O   T F O   T F O   K F Q T   U F D L

6. K D J G Y Y   W F F W P Y

7. L N Y   S L A K   U S L A K   A I S W Y T

8. N F G Y K   I F G Y K

9. S Z   D   P S L L P Y   L Y D I F L

10. T S J V   D T F Q J W   L N Y   T F A S Y

53

PUZZLE #72: PATRIOTIC SONGS

Crypto-lists are lists of related words and phrases that have been translated into a code. The code is the same for every word in the list. For example, if G represents A in one word, it will represent A in every word on the list. Your job is to find the right code so that every word fits the theme of this puzzle.

NAME

HINT: Start thinking of answers that might fit the theme and try out that code. Or you can start by looking for common words that have the same letter pattern. Not every letter of the alphabet will be used in the puzzle.

ORIGINAL LETTER REPRESENTS

A	B	C	D	E	F	G	H	I	J	K	L	M

N	O	P	Q	R	S	T	U	V	W	X	Y	Z

1 K T W ▓ Q B H N N ▓ I Y H S Z A I

2 Y C ▓ A T J P R S C ▓ R Z N ▓ T O ▓ R V H H

3 C T J S H ▓ I ▓ K S I P W ▓ T B W ▓ O B I K

4 C I P E H H ▓ W T T W B H ▓ W I P W C

5 K T W ▓ Q B H N N ▓ R V H ▓ J N I

6 R V Z N ▓ Z N ▓ Y C ▓ A T J P R S C

7 N R I S ▓ N M I P K B H W ▓ Q I P P H S

8 I Y H S Z A I ▓ R V H ▓ Q H I J R Z O J B

9 R V Z N ▓ B I P W ▓ Z N ▓ C T J S ▓ B I P W

SECTION 7
MUSICAL CODES

PUZZLE #73: MUSICAL INSTRUMENTS

Musical Codes are lists of related words and phrases that have been translated into a code. The code is the same for every word in the list. For example, if 7 represents A in one word, it will represent A in every word on the list. Your job is to substitute the given letter for each number.

NUMBER REPRESENTS

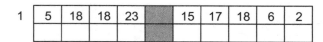

1	2	3	4	5	6	7	8	9	10	11	12	13
E	K	P	T	W	C	R	Z	G	A	M	I	V

14	15	16	17	18	19	20	21	22	23	24	25	26
Y	B	F	L	O	U	H	Q	J	D	X	N	S

1. 5 18 18 23 ▓ 15 17 18 6 2

2. 9 17 18 6 2 1 25 26 3 12 1 17

3. 8 12 4 20 1 7

4. 16 17 19 4 1

5. 26 10 24 18 3 20 18 25 1

6. 6 14 11 15 10 17 26

7. 2 1 4 4 17 1 ▓ 23 7 19 11

8. 15 10 25 22 18

9. 13 12 18 17 12 25

10. 24 14 17 18 3 20 18 25 1

PUZZLE #74:   COMPOSERS

Musical Codes are lists of related words and phrases that have been translated into a code. The code is the same for every word in the list. For example, if 7 represents A in one word, it will represent A in every word on the list. Your job is to substitute the given letter for each number.

NUMBER REPRESENTS

1	2	3	4	5	6	7	8	9	10	11	12	13
D	K	W	P	G	A	M	T	V	R	I	B	E

14	15	16	17	18	19	20	21	22	23	24	25	26
N	Y	O	F	Q	Z	S	J	C	H	U	X	L

1 | 5 | 13 | 10 | 20 | 23 | 3 | 11 | 14 |

2 | 1 | 9 | 16 | 10 | 6 | 2 |

3 | 12 | 13 | 10 | 14 | 20 | 8 | 13 | 11 | 14 |

4 | 7 | 16 | 19 | 6 | 10 | 8 |

5 | 20 | 16 | 14 | 1 | 23 | 13 | 11 | 7 |

6 | 22 | 16 | 4 | 26 | 6 | 14 | 1 |

7 | 8 | 22 | 23 | 6 | 11 | 2 | 16 | 9 | 20 | 2 | 15 |

8 | 21 | 16 | 4 | 26 | 11 | 14 |

9 | 1 | 13 | 12 | 24 | 20 | 20 | 15 |

10 | 17 | 6 | 24 | 10 | 13 |

PUZZLE #75:   ITALIAN MUSICAL TERMS

Musical Codes are lists of related words and phrases that have been translated into a code. The code is the same for every word in the list. For example, if 7 represents A in one word, it will represent A in every word on the list. Your job is to substitute the given letter for each number.

NUMBER REPRESENTS

1	2	3	4	5	6	7	8	9	10	11	12	13
V	M	E	H	R	X	P	B	F	K	T	Z	C

14	15	16	17	18	19	20	21	22	23	24	25	26
J	O	U	G	A	S	Q	Y	L	D	I	N	W

1. | 17 | 22 | 24 | 19 | 19 | 18 | 25 | 23 | 15 |
|---|---|---|---|---|---|---|---|---|
| | | | | | | | | |

2. | 7 | 24 | 12 | 12 | 24 | 13 | 18 | 11 | 15 |
|---|---|---|---|---|---|---|---|---|
| | | | | | | | | |

3. | 9 | 3 | 5 | 2 | 18 | 11 | 18 |
|---|---|---|---|---|---|---|
| | | | | | | |

4. | 11 | 5 | 18 | 25 | 20 | 16 | 24 | 22 | 22 | 15 |
|---|---|---|---|---|---|---|---|---|---|
| | | | | | | | | | |

5. | 13 | 18 | 23 | 3 | 25 | 12 | 18 |
|---|---|---|---|---|---|---|
| | | | | | | |

6. | 18 | 5 | 7 | 3 | 17 | 17 | 24 | 15 |
|---|---|---|---|---|---|---|---|
| | | | | | | | |

7. | 19 | 9 | 15 | 5 | 12 | 18 | 25 | 23 | 15 |
|---|---|---|---|---|---|---|---|---|
| | | | | | | | | |

8. | 18 | 13 | 18 | 7 | 7 | 3 | 22 | 22 | 18 |
|---|---|---|---|---|---|---|---|---|
| | | | | | | | | |

9. | 1 | 24 | 8 | 5 | 18 | 11 | 15 |
|---|---|---|---|---|---|---|
| | | | | | | |

10. | 2 | 18 | 3 | 19 | 11 | 5 | 15 |
|---|---|---|---|---|---|---|
| | | | | | | |

PUZZLE #76: OPERAS

Musical Codes are lists of related words and phrases that have been translated into a code. The code is the same for every word in the list. For example, if 7 represents A in one word, it will represent A in every word on the list. Your job is to substitute the given letter for each number.

NUMBER REPRESENTS

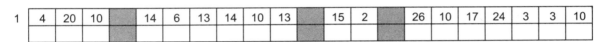

1	2	3	4	5	6	7	8	9	10	11	12	13
Y	F	L	T	Q	A	G	M	U	E	P	J	R

14	15	16	17	18	19	20	21	22	23	24	25	26
B	O	K	V	C	X	H	N	D	Z	I	W	S

1. 4 20 10 ▓ 14 6 13 14 10 13 ▓ 15 2 ▓ 26 10 17 24 3 3 10

2. 11 6 7 3 24 6 18 18 24

3. 3 6 ▓ 4 13 6 17 24 6 4 6

4. 18 6 13 8 10 21

5. 22 15 21 ▓ 7 24 15 17 6 21 21 24

6. 4 20 10 ▓ 8 6 7 24 18 ▓ 2 3 9 4 10

7. 4 20 10 ▓ 8 6 13 13 24 6 7 10 ▓ 15 2 ▓ 2 24 7 6 13 15

8. 4 15 26 18 6

9. 13 24 7 15 3 10 4 4 15

10. 6 24 22 6

SECTION 8
SCRAMBLED WORDS

PUZZLE #77: BROADWAY MUSICALS

_____

NAME

The left column contains scrambled Broadway musical titles. Your job is to unscramble the titles and write the correct word in the right column.

Some of the letters in the new word have a number underneath them. Write the letter in the corresponding blank at the bottom of the page.

If you do this correctly, you should have found four additional Broadway musical titles.

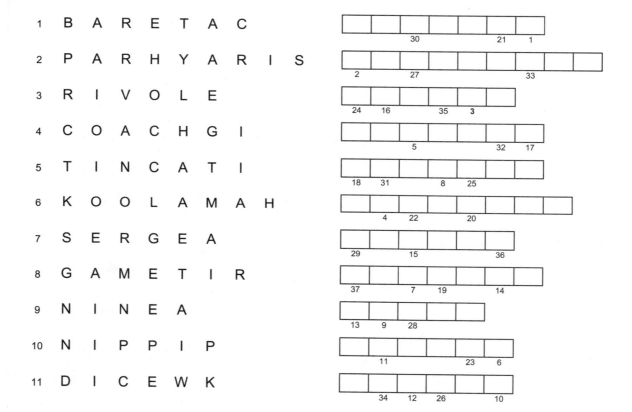

1 B A R E T A C

2 P A R H Y A R I S

3 R I V O L E

4 C O A C H G I

5 T I N C A T I

6 K O O L A M A H

7 S E R G E A

8 G A M E T I R

9 N I N E A

10 N I P P I P

11 D I C E W K

BONUS WORDS

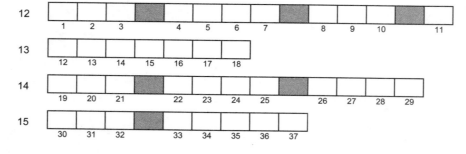

12 — 1 2 3 _ 4 5 6 7 _ 8 9 10 _ 11

13 — 12 13 14 15 16 17 18

14 — 19 20 21 _ 22 23 24 25 _ 26 27 28 29

15 — 30 31 32 _ 33 34 35 36 37

PUZZLE #78: MUSICAL INSTRUMENTS

The left column contains scrambled musical instrument names. Your job is to unscramble the musical instrument and write the correct word in the right column.

Some of the letters in the new word have a number underneath them. Write the letter in the corresponding blank at the bottom of the page.

If you do this correctly, you should have found four additional musical instrument names.

NAME

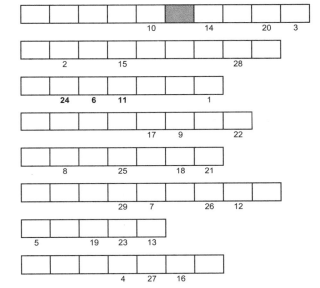

1   R E D M U N R A S

2   P H A X O N S E O

3   P U T T E R M

4   R I C A L N T E

5   P A I N T I M

6   I N C R O C A D A

7   G R O A N

8   B A L S M Y C

BONUS WORDS

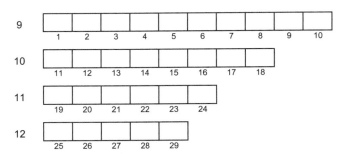

9

10

11

12

PUZZLE #79: MUSICAL TERMS

_____

NAME

The left column contains scrambled musical terms. Your job is to unscramble the term and write the correct word in the right column.

Some of the letters in the new word have a number underneath them. Write the letter in the corresponding blank at the bottom of the page.

If you do this correctly, you should have found four additional musical terms.

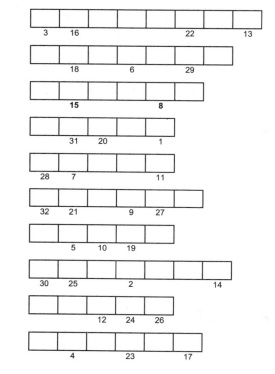

1 S O M E C R O P

2 R E A S U M E

3 C O R N E E

4 L O G A R

5 D U E T E

6 T E A L O G

7 P O E T M

8 T R I B A V O

9 N O T B A

10 M Y R T H H

BONUS WORDS

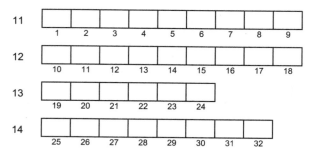

11

12

13

14

SECTION 9
WORD SEARCHES

PUZZLE #80:   MUSICAL TERMS

Find the musical terms listed below in the grid. The words in the grid may be forward, backward, up, down, or diagonal. Each word will always be in a straight line. Circle or highlight the word.

NAME

```
C  M  Y  E  N  R  U  T  C  O  N  A  C  B
O  M  H  D  I  T  E  N  O  R  L  H  A  P
N  A  E  T  O  N  I  J  V  T  O  T  E  B
D  E  R  T  Y  L  S  B  O  R  O  R  E  T
U  S  L  E  R  H  E  T  D  N  C  A  A  O
C  P  S  A  P  O  R  M  R  U  T  L  X  O
T  R  O  B  C  O  F  C  S  U  F  D  O  P
O  A  N  S  P  S  O  S  V  C  M  Z  J  M
R  H  G  I  H  M  I  E  G  O  H  E  M  E
H  S  A  C  P  O  V  N  C  M  L  O  N  T
U  N  R  O  N  A  I  I  C  S  E  U  I  T
O  A  S  H  T  R  S  S  V  O  S  T  M  R
M  E  V  C  T  U  N  O  T  E  D  A  E  E
R  N  O  S  M  S  C  O  R  E  R  A  B  R
```

ALTO	CONDUCTOR	NOCTURNE	SCORE
BASS	FLAT	NOTE	SHARP
BATON	FORTE	OCTAVE	SONG
BEAT	INSTRUMENT	OPERA	STRING
CHOIR	MARCH	PERCUSSION	TEMPO
CHORD	MELODY	PIANO	TENOR
CODA	METER	RHYTHM	VOLUME
COMPOSER	MUSIC	SCALE	

PUZZLE #81: MUSICAL INSTRUMENTS

Find the musical instruments listed below in the grid. The words in the grid may be forward, backward, up, down, or diagonal. Each word will always be in a straight line. Circle or highlight the word.

NAME _____

```
E  O  C  L  A  R  I  N  E  T  B  G  N  B
E  L  G  D  R  U  M  X  I  U  U  R  A  X
N  P  D  N  E  O  B  O  G  I  O  S  N  Y
O  I  D  D  O  D  Q  L  T  H  S  A  T  L
H  C  P  R  I  B  E  A  H  O  G  H  E  O
P  C  R  K  O  F  R  C  O  R  A  O  P  P
O  O  A  U  C  H  N  N  O  F  V  R  M  H
X  L  H  H  O  E  C  S  N  O  L  N  U  O
A  O  I  J  R  T  Q  I  L  I  L  U  R  N
S  M  N  F  E  V  C  O  S  A  L  L  T  E
E  A  C  N  T  U  B  A  N  P  B  O  E  E
B  T  R  O  M  G  N  O  G  A  R  M  I  C
C  O  E  N  O  B  M  O  R  T  I  A  Y  V
C  C  A  S  T  A  N  E  T  S  C  P  H  C
```

BANJO	CLARINET	GONG	PIANO
BASSOON	CORNET	GUITAR	PICCOLO
BONGO	CYMBALS	HARP	SAXOPHONE
BUGLE	DRUM	HARPSICHORD	TROMBONE
CASTANETS	FIDDLE	HORN	TRUMPET
CELLO	FLUTE	OBOE	TUBA
CHIME	FRENCH HORN	ORGAN	VIOLIN
			XYLOPHONE

PUZZLE #82: COMPOSERS

Find the names of the composers listed below in the grid.
The words in the grid may be forward, backward, up, down,
or diagonal. Each word will always be in a straight line.
Circle or highlight the word.

NAME _____

```
C  D  T  V  I  V  A  L  D  I  M  T  D  B
M  O  N  S  W  L  E  V  A  R  E  V  R  B
A  A  P  E  L  B  A  C  H  Z  O  A  E  S
B  P  H  L  V  O  A  N  I  R  H  R  S  C
I  R  I  L  A  O  H  B  A  M  N  Q  T  H
N  E  D  J  E  N  H  K  S  S  K  R  R  U
I  T  R  H  J  R  D  T  T  X  E  E  A  B
C  R  E  S  L  N  B  E  E  H  R  N  U  E
N  O  V  I  I  E  I  H  N  E  N  G  S  R
A  P  S  L  R  N  A  A  A  I  B  A  S  T
M  Z  P  L  S  O  U  S  A  N  P  W  F  M
T  O  I  A  T  R  A  Z  O  M  D  O  X  J
J  O  D  E  B  U  S  S  Y  U  N  E  H  U
Z  G  E  R  S  H  W  I  N  L  Y  E  L  C
```

BACH	COPLAND	KERN	SCHUBERT
BEETHOVEN	DEBUSSY	LISZT	SOUSA
BERLIOZ	DVORAK	MAHLER	STRAUSS
BERNSTEIN	GERSHWIN	MANCINI	VERDI
BIZET	HANDEL	MOZART	VIVALDI
BRAHMS	HOLST	PORTER	WAGNER
CHOPIN	JOPLIN	RAVEL	

PUZZLE #83: BROADWAY MUSICALS

Find the names of the Broadway musicals listed below in the grid. The words in the grid may be forward, backward, up, down, or diagonal. Each word will always be in a straight line. Circle or highlight the word.

NAME _____

```
C  H  O  R  U  S  L  I  N  E  E  J  Y  T  S  P
K  E  I  M  A  M  M  A  M  I  A  R  E  M  O  O
I  P  I  G  R  E  A  S  E  T  O  R  K  Y  U  R
S  R  S  N  I  M  B  Q  I  T  A  S  I  F  T  G
S  O  R  E  N  T  N  V  S  B  U  R  N  A  H  Y
M  D  Z  U  L  A  E  E  A  E  G  I  G  I  P  A
E  U  P  D  U  B  D  C  B  Z  B  A  A  R  A  N
K  C  A  T  S  I  A  L  L  J  U  H  N  L  C  D
A  E  F  L  S  D  N  R  R  T  C  I  D  A  I  B
T  R  P  T  E  H  I  W  E  I  O  U  I  D  F  E
E  S  S  K  W  A  D  I  A  S  G  L  L  Y  I  S
K  E  C  O  M  P  A  N  Y  W  I  Y  E  M  C  S
W  I  H  A  I  R  S  P  R  A  Y  M  N  M  H  E
W  Z  Y  L  L  O  D  O  L  L  E  H  S  N  A  H
A  C  I  S  U  M  F  O  D  N  U  O  S  E  U  C
E  V  S  L  L  O  D  D  N  A  S  Y  U  G  L  F
```

AIDA	COMPANY	HAIRSPRAY	PORGY AND BESS
ANNIE	EVITA	HELLO DOLLY	PRODUCERS
CABARET	FUNNY GIRL	KING AND I	RENT
CAMELOT	GIGI	KISS ME KATE	SOUND OF MUSIC
CATS	GREASE	LES MISERABLES	SOUTH PACIFIC
CHESS	GUYS AND DOLLS	MAMMA MIA	WEST SIDE STORY
CHORUS LINE	HAIR	MY FAIR LADY	WICKED

PUZZLE #84:   ITALIAN MUSICAL TERMS

Find the Italian musical terms listed below in the grid. The words in the grid may be forward, backward, up, down, or diagonal. Each word will always be in a straight line. Circle or highlight the word.

NAME _____

```
L   P   A   A   T   A   M   R   E   F   O   D
A   E   M   D   Q   E   U   M   I   N   O   O
L   R   G   A   O   G   N   N   A   L   M   A
L   O   D   A   E   C   E   I   C   I   R   N
E   T   R   C   T   S   P   E   S   L   O   D
G   A   A   N   Y   O   T   S   U   E   T   A
R   M   T   O   O   A   I   O   Q   N   S   N
O   I   I   G   D   N   M   E   S   T   E   T
F   N   R   A   A   D   M   Z   T   O   R   E
U   A   G   I   O   T   A   B   U   R   P   S
L   I   P   O   T   A   C   R   A   M   O   Z
O   O   R   O   T   A   C   C   A   T   S   F
```

ADAGIO	FINE	PIANISSIMO
ALLEGRO	FORTE	PIANO
ANDANTE	LARGO	PRESTO
ANIMATO	LEGATO	RITARD
CODA	LENTO	RUBATO
DOLCE	MAESTOSO	STACCATO
FERMATA	MARCATO	

PUZZLE #85:   KINDS OF MUSICAL WORKS

NAME _____

Find the musical works listed below in the grid. The words in the grid may be forward, backward, up, down, or diagonal. Each word will always be in a straight line. Circle or highlight the word.

```
A  S  S  G  E  C  V  O  K  O  Y
N  O  H  Y  X  U  T  F  L  Z  T
T  N  Y  F  M  R  G  W  O  T  E
H  A  M  J  E  P  C  U  F  L  U
E  T  N  C  S  M  H  A  F  A  N
M  A  N  E  E  M  O  O  N  W  I
C  O  U  D  A  A  N  T  N  O  M
C  L  U  R  R  W  L  Y  E  Y  N
B  T  C  E  D  A  I  R  A  T  B
E  H  P  F  A  N  F  A  R  E  F
R  O  C  H  O  R  A  L  E  W  Y
```

ANTHEM	FUGUE
ARIA	HYMN
BLUES	MARCH
CANON	MINUET
CHORALE	MOTET
CONCERTO	OPERA
ETUDE	SONATA
FANFARE	SYMPHONY
FOLK	WALTZ

PUZZLE #36: JAZZ LEGENDS

Find the first and last names of the jazz legends listed below in the grid. The words in the grid may be forward, backward, up, down, or diagonal. Each word will always be in a straight line. Circle or highlight the word.

_____

NAME

```
G  N  D  C  H  A  R  L  I  E  D  C  V  H  K
Y  N  A  I  B  I  L  L  H  V  O  Y  E  C  T
F  A  O  M  Z  H  C  I  R  U  N  R  O  H  H
E  B  D  R  D  Z  T  N  N  B  C  F  S  E
N  J  A  I  T  O  Y  T  E  I  N  I  N  Q  L
A  N  J  S  L  S  O  B  E  A  T  B  A  A  O
R  K  O  Z  I  O  M  G  H  Z  S  Z  T  L  N
T  N  H  J  A  E  H  R  G  Y  S  E  S  L  I
L  O  N  P  S  R  B  E  A  B  Y  I  L  E  U
O  M  U  I  E  R  R  V  K  K  I  D  V  I  S
C  R  U  K  U  A  E  M  F  S  E  L  D  A  M
K  O  R  B  L  N  E  V  A  D  N  N  L  U  D
L  A  E  D  E  L  A  E  K  U  D  A  T  I  B
P  C  L  G  I  L  L  E  S  P  I  E  V  O  E
K  X  E  J  N  O  T  G  N  I  L  L  E  E  N
```

FIRST NAME	LAST NAME	FIRST NAME	LAST NAME
LOUIS	ARMSTRONG	BENNY	GOODMAN
COUNT	BASIE	HERBIE	HANCOCK
DAVE	BRUBECK	BILLIE	HOLIDAY
JOHN	COLTRANE	STAN	KENTON
MILES	DAVIS	GENE	KRUPA
DUKE	ELLINGTON	THELONIUS	MONK
BILL	EVANS	CHARLIE	PARKER
ELLA	FITZGERALD	BUDDY	RICH
DIZZY	GILLESPIE		

SECTION 10
KRISS KROSS

PUZZLE #87: ITALIAN MUSICAL TERMS

Place the words into the grid in crossword fashion, either across or down. Cross off the words as you use them, since each will be used exactly one time. HINT: Start with the only 9 letter word.

NAME

4 LETTERS	5 LETTERS	6 LETTERS	7 LETTERS	8 LETTERS	9 LETTERS	10 LETTERS	11 LETTERS
CODA	DOLCE	ADAGIO	ALLEGRO	ARPEGGIO	CRESCENDO	PIANISSIMO	ACCELERANDO
FINE	FORTE	LEGATO	ANDANTE	MAESTOSO		RITARDANDO	DECRESCENDO
	LARGO	PRESTO	ANIMATO	MODERATO			
		VIVACE	FERMATA	STACCATO			
			MARCATO				

74

PUZZLE #88: KINDS OF MUSICAL WORKS

Place the words into the grid in crossword fashion, either across or down. Cross off the words as you use them, since each will be used exactly one time. HINT: Start with the two 6 letter words.

NAME

4 LETTERS	5 LETTERS	6 LETTERS	7 LETTERS	8 LETTERS
ARIA	CANON	ANTHEM	CANTATA	CONCERTO
DUET	ETUDE	SONATA	CHORALE	NOCTURNE
SOLO	FUGUE		FANFARE	ORATORIO
	MOTET			RHAPSODY
	OCTET			SERENADE
	OPERA			SYMPHONY
	ROUND			
	WALTZ			

PUZZLE #89:   COMPOSERS—NOW & THEN

Place the words into the grid in crossword fashion, either across or down. Cross off the words as you use them, since each will be used exactly one time. HINT: Start with the only 10 letter word.

NAME

4 LETTERS	**5 LETTERS**	**6 LETTERS**	**7 LETTERS**	**8 LETTERS**	**9 LETTERS**	**10 LETTERS**	**11 LETTERS**
BACH	BIZET	BARTOK	BERLIOZ	GERSHWIN	BEETHOVEN	STRAVINSKY	RACHMANINOV
IVES	GRIEG	BERLIN	COPLAND	SCHUBERT	BERNSTEIN		TCHAIKOVSKY
KERN	HAYDN	BRAHMS	DEBUSSY	WILLIAMS	PROKOFIEV		
	LISZT	CHOPIN	MANCINI				
	RAVEL	DVORAK	PUCCINI				
	SOUSA	GOUNOD	RODGERS				
	VERDI	HANDEL	ROSSINI				
		MAHLER	STRAUSS				
		MOZART	VIVALDI				
		PORTER					

PUZZLE #90: MUSICAL INSTRUMENTS

Place the words into the grid in crossword fashion, either across or down. Cross off the words as you use them, since each will be used exactly one time. HINT: Start with the only 9 or 10 letter word.

NAME

4 LETTERS	5 LETTERS	6 LETTERS	7 LETTERS	8 LETTERS	9 LETTERS	10 LETTERS
DRUM	BANJO	CORNET	BASSOON	CLARINET	SAXOPHONE	TAMBOURINE
FIFE	BUGLE	FIDDLE	CYMBALS	TROMBONE		
GONG	CELLO	GUITAR	PICCOLO			
HARP	CHIME	VIOLIN	TIMPANI			
LUTE	FLUTE		TRUMPET			
OBOE	PIANO					
TUBA	VIOLA					

PUZZLE #91: BROADWAY MUSICALS

Place the words into the grid in crossword fashion, either across or down. Cross off the words as you use them, since each will be used exactly one time. HINT: Start with the only 10 letter word.

_____

NAME

4 LETTERS	**5 LETTERS**	**6 LETTERS**	**7 LETTERS**	**8 LETTERS**	**9 LETTERS**	**10 LETTERS**
CATS	ANNIE	OLIVER	CABARET	CAROUSEL	BRIGADOON	DREAMGIRLS
GIGI	EVITA	PIPPIN	CAMELOT	OKLAHOMA	HAIRSPRAY	
MAME		WICKED	CANDIDE			
			RAGTIME			
			TITANIC			

PUZZLE #92: MUSICAL TERMS

Place the words into the grid in crossword fashion, either across or down. Cross off the words as you use them, since each will be used exactly one time. HINT: Start with the only 10 letter word.

NAME

WARNING: This one is TOUGH!

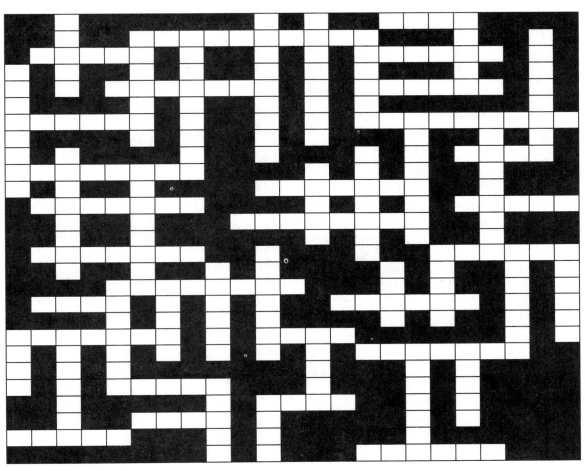

4 LETTERS	5 LETTERS	6 LETTERS	7 LETTERS	8 LETTERS	9 LETTERS	10 LETTERS
ALTO	BATON	ACCENT	ANDANTE	COMPOSER	CRESCENDO	ACCIDENTAL
BASS	BRASS	ANTHEM	BAR LINE	CONCERTO	METRONOME	
CLEF	CHORD	CHORUS	FANFARE	DYNAMICS	ORCHESTRA	
CODA	FORTE	ENCORE	FERMATA	INTERVAL	SFORZANDO	
FLAT	LARGO	LEGATO	HARMONY	NOCTURNE		
NOTE	METER	OCTAVE	MAESTRO	OVERTURE		
REST	OPERA	RHYTHM	MEASURE	RHAPSODY		
SONG	PIANO	RITARD	NATURAL	STACCATO		
STEM	RANGE	STANZA	RECITAL	SYMPHONY		
	SCALE		REFRAIN			
	SHARP		SOPRANO			
	TENOR		STRINGS			
			TRIPLET			

SECTION 11
COMPLETE THE STORY

PUZZLE #93: THE ABE BRADY STORY

_____

NAME

Fill in the blanks with the Treble Clef note names in the musical exercise on the following page. The measure numbers match the word numbers below.

This is the story of (1)_ _ _ Brady, a mythical lumberjack, and his great ox, (2)_ _ _ _. (3) _ _ _ was so big that when his (4)_ _ _ built a (5)_ _ _ for him it was as long as a soccer field and as wide as a (6)_ _ _ _ for 43 lions. The (7)_ _ _ _ of the (8)_ _ _ was so high that it took 102 sacks of ox (9)_ _ _ _ to build the steps so (10)_ _ _ could get into (11)_ _ _ at night.

(12)_ _ _ _ wore a (13)_ _ _ _ _ with a (14)_ _ _ _ border, saying that he was not to (15)_ _ (16)_ _ _ any (17)_ _ _ _ _ _ _ , no matter how much he (18) _ _ _ _ _ _ . You know, of course, that (19) _ _ _ sandwiches and (20)_ _ _ _ _ _ _ were Babe's favorite foods.

One day, (21)_ _ _ decided to take a trip. He called for a (22)_ _ _ , which, because he was so big, needed to be the size of a truck. (23)_ _ _ loaded his shoulder (24) _ _ _ and (25)_ _ _ _ _ _ _ , and then told the (26) _ _ _ driver to take him to the (27)_ _ _ _ _ _ (28)_ _ _ _ , where the (29) _ _ _ Four and the Grateful (30)_ _ _ _ were giving a concert.

After the concert, (31)_ _ _ had a dinner which included (32)_ _ _ _ stew and biscuits with (33)_ _ _ honey. He was so hungry that the cook (34)_ _ _ _ _ more (35)_ _ _ _ and vegetables. (36)_ _ _ was still hungry, so he asked if he could have a (37)_ _ _ of ice cream. Now for big (38)_ _ _ , a (39) _ _ _ of anything was enough to open a store. The ice cream was served in three wheelbarrows, each containing a different flavor. "(40)_ _ _," (41) _ _ _ said, "Where is the chocolate sauce?"

(42)_ _ _ was a lumberjack, which means he cut down trees. The best trees were on the (43)_ _ _ _ of the mountain. (44)_ _ _ did not want to cut down all the trees, so he had to (45)_ _ _ _ the (46)_ _ _ of the trees and only cut down the most (47)_ _ _ _ ones. His axe was so big that when he swung it, he chopped down 15 trees at a time. This made so much noise that even the (48)_ _ _ _ could hear the trees fall.

PUZZLE #93: THE ABE BRADY STORY

NAME

PUZZLE #94:   THE TRIP WITH MY FATHER

_____

Fill in the blanks with the Bass Clef note names in the musical exercise on the following page. The measure numbers match the word numbers below.

NAME

For many years my father traveled on business trips, but I had never gone anywhere. "(1)_ _ _, (2) _ _ _, why can't you do a good (3) _ _ _ _ and take me along? I just (4)_ _ _ _ my math test, so this would be a great reward for me." I (5)_ _ _ _ _ _ and pleaded, but it seemed as though he was (6)_ _ _ _ since he kept ignoring me. Then, with a grin on his (7)_ _ _ _, he said "Put (8) _ _ _. 21st on your calendar, and we will go."

When that day came, we loaded our (9)_ _ _ _ _ _ _ into a (10)_ _ _ and were off to the airport. On the plane, I was on the (11)_ _ _ _ of my seat with excitement. The only thing (12)_ _ _ about the flight was that they didn't (13)_ _ _ _ me anything but a (14)_ _ _ of peanuts.

Once we landed, Dad took me to an outdoor (15)_ _ _ _. They had lots of (16) _ _ _ dishes on the menu, so Dad ordered an omelet. I ordered corned (17)_ _ _ _ and (18)_ _ _ _ _ _ _. While we were waiting for our food, (19) _ _ _ kept talking about the building with the beautiful (20)_ _ _ _ _ _ across the street. I was more interested in the nearby (21)_ _ _ _ _ parrot that (22)_ _ _ _ _ me and tried to (23)_ _ _ with me.

After we were (24)_ _ _, we had a full day of touring. I went (25) _ _ _ _ over some of the sights we saw and things we experienced. At the end of the day, I couldn't (26)_ _ _ _ how many miles we had walked, but as the sunlight (27)_ _ _ _ _, even at my (28) _ _ _, I was (29) _ _ _ _ tired and (30)_ _ _ _ _ _ to go to bed early.

PUZZLE #94: **THE TRIP WITH MY FATHER**

NAME

SECTION 12
BUILDING BLOCKS

PUZZLE #95: BUILDING BLOCKS A

There are four building blocks. Each one has six sides.

Each of the blocks has a single letter of the alphabet on each side.

By arranging the blocks in various ways, you can spell all of the words below.

Can you figure out how the letters are arranged on the four blocks? Q and Z are not used on the blocks.

NAME

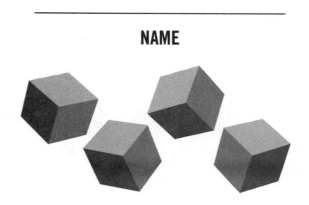

ALTO	EXIT	NOTE	REST
BACH	JIVE	OVAL	SHOW
BEAT	KATE	PATH	SOFT
DING	LOUD	PLAY	TONE
DRUM			

Cross off the letters as you use them.

A B C D E F G H I J K L M N O P Q R S T U V W X Y Z

BLOCK 1	BLOCK 2	BLOCK 3	BLOCK 4
1 A	1 L	1 T	1 O
2	2	2	2
3	3	3	3
4	4	4	4
5	5	5	5
6	6	6	6

PUZZLE #96:   BUILDING BLOCKS B

There are four building blocks. Each one has six sides.

Each of the blocks has a single letter of the alphabet on each side.

By arranging the blocks in various ways, you can spell all of the words below.

Can you figure out how the letters are arranged on the four blocks? X and Y are not used on the blocks.

NAME _____

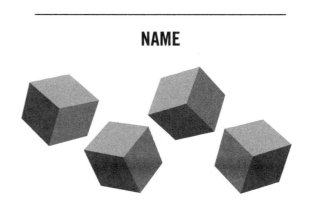

BAND	HARP	QUIT	STEP
CLEF	HORN	QUIZ	TUBA
DRUM	JUST	SOFT	VAST
FLAT	LUTE	SONG	WISH
FRET	PICK		

Cross off the letters as you use them.

A B C D E F G H I J K L M N O P Q R S T U V W X Y Z

BLOCK 1	BLOCK 2	BLOCK 3	BLOCK 4
1 B	1 A	1 N	1 D
2	2	2	2
3	3	3	3
4	4	4	4
5	5	5	5
6	6	6	6

PUZZLE #97:   BUILDING BLOCKS C

There are four building blocks. Each one has six sides.

Each of the blocks has a single letter of the alphabet on each side.

By arranging the blocks in various ways, you can spell all of the words below.

Can you figure out how the letters are arranged on the four blocks? J and X are not used on the blocks.

NAME

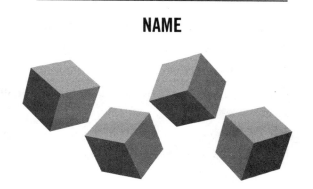

BEAT	FAIR	LOUD	SIDE
BLOW	FINE	PACK	SONG
BOAT	HARP	PLAY	TUNE
CATS	HYMN	QUIZ	WEST
DUET	IVES	SHOW	ZEST

Cross off the letters as you use them.

A B C D E F G H I J K L M N O P Q R S T U V W X Y Z

BLOCK 1	**BLOCK 2**	**BLOCK 3**	**BLOCK 4**
1 B	1 E	1 A	1 T
2	2	2	2
3	3	3	3
4	4	4	4
5	5	5	5
6	6	6	6

PUZZLE #98: BUILDING BLOCKS D

There are four building blocks. Each one has six sides.

Each of the blocks has a single letter of the alphabet on each side.

By arranging the blocks in various ways, you can spell all of the words below.

Can you figure out how the letters are arranged on the four blocks? Q and X are not used on the blocks.

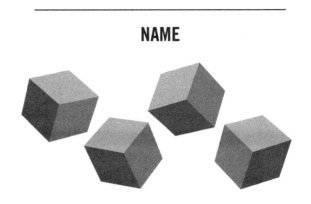

NAME _____

ALTO	DRUM	JUST	STEP
CLEF	FLAT	KITE	TUBA
CODA	HARP	LUTE	VOLT
CUES	HAZY	LYRE	WALK
DUET	HORN	SONG	

Cross off the letters as you use them.

A B C D E F G H I J K L M N O P Q R S T U V W X Y Z

	BLOCK 1		BLOCK 2		BLOCK 3		BLOCK 4
1	A	1	L	1	T	1	O
2		2		2		2	
3		3		3		3	
4		4		4		4	
5		5		5		5	
6		6		6		6	

SECTION 13
BUILD-A-WORD

PUZZLE #99: #1-4

NAME

Hidden in each box on this page are five words. One word is the name of a musical category. The other 4 words are members of that category.

For example, if the category was Percussion, you would find 4 types of percussion instruments. To form a word, start by choosing one block from column A. Then choose a block from columns B, C, D, and E in order. You may want to cross off a block as you use it, since each block will only be used one time. Write the name of the category on the "CAT" line. Underneath, write the names of the other 4 words.

#1

	A	B	C	D	E
	C	EN	N	P	ET
	B	U	M	E	RN
	FR	R	A	HO	E
	B	OR	G	L	S
	TR	U	CH	S	T

CAT _____
1 _____
2 _____
3 _____
4 _____

#2

	A	B	C	D	E
	C	I	L	N	E
	GU	T	D	L	N
	VI	ID	RI	A	O
	F	E	L	I	GS
	S	O	T	L	R

CAT _____
1 _____
2 _____
3 _____
4 _____

#3

	A	B	C	D	E
	BA	L	OP	IN	NE
	PI	O	SO	L	E
	F	X	CO	T	DS
	SA	S	DW	HO	N
	WO	C	U	O	O

CAT _____
1 _____
2 _____
3 _____
4 _____

#4

	A	B	C	D	E
	B	M	A	AN	E
	D	N	U	G	S
	D	O	P	B	E
	S	JE	N	M	I
	TI	R	M	R	O

CAT _____
1 _____
2 _____
3 _____
4 _____

PUZZLE #100: #5-8

NAME _____

Hidden in each box on this page are five words. One word is the name of a musical category. The other 4 words are members of that category.

For example, if the category was Percussion, you would find 4 types of percussion instruments. To form a word, start by choosing one block from column A. Then choose a block from columns B, C, D, and E in order. You may want to cross off a block as you use it, since each block will only be used one time. Write the name of the category on the "CAT" line. Underneath, write the names of the other 4 words.

#5

	A	B	C	D	E
	AN	E	LE	T	RO
	P	L	R	S	O
	T	A	N	G	E
	A	DA	E	P	TO
	L	R	M	G	O

CAT _____
1 _____
2 _____
3 _____
4 _____

#6

	A	B	C	D	E
	A	S	S	A	D
	G	IR	N	KE	LS
	HA	I	IC	I	AY
	MU	N	E	PR	SE
	W	R	C	A	E

CAT _____
1 _____
2 _____
3 _____
4 _____

#7

	A	B	C	D	E
	P	FO	CE	N	DO
	CR	O	M	AN	O
	S	I	R	I	E
	DY	ES	A	ND	CS
	F	NA	RZ	T	O

CAT _____
1 _____
2 _____
3 _____
4 _____

#8

	A	B	C	D	E
	CO	I	H	E	S
	M	AN	O	A	T
	H	O	Z	M	L
	BR	MP	Z	E	RS
	B	A	D	SE	RT

CAT _____
1 _____
2 _____
3 _____
4 _____

SECTION 14
MAZES

(BY CHRISTOPHER BRADEN)

PUZZLE #101: MAZES - PIANO

NAME

Have a grand time finding your way through this maze.
Patience is the key to your success.

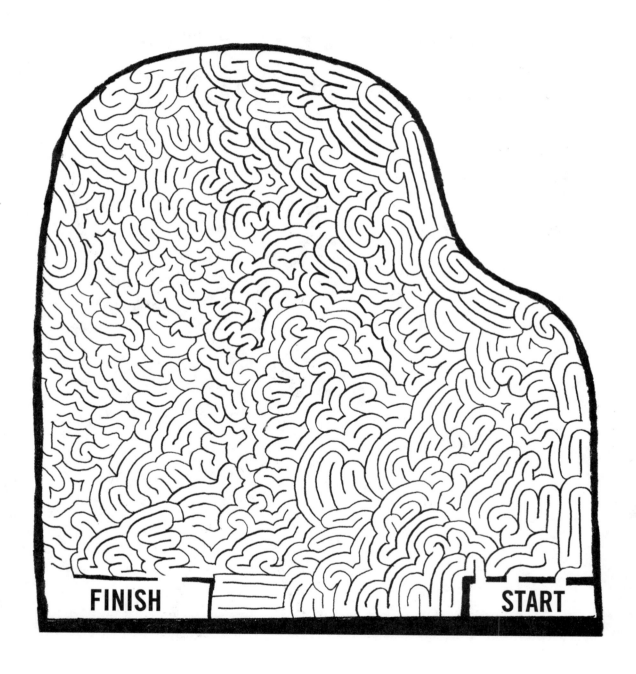

FINISH

START

PUZZLE BONUS: MAZES - MARACAS

Shake it up! Easy does it as you get a handle on this challenging maze.

_____

NAME

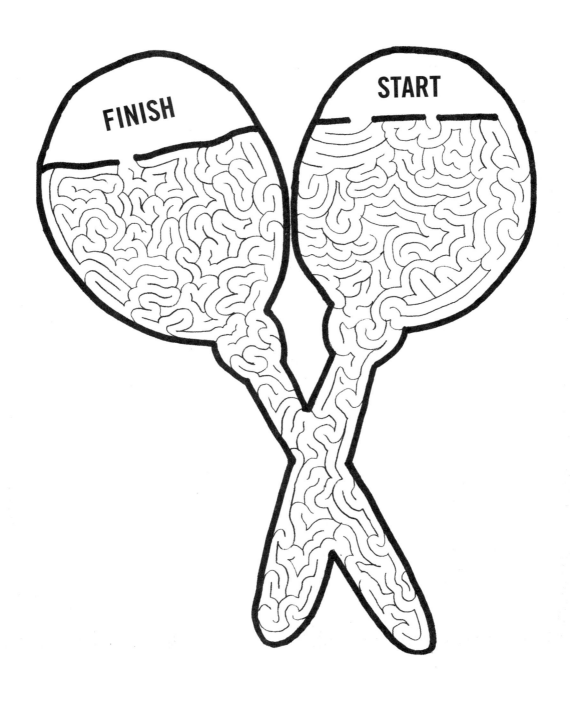

ANSWER KEYS

PUZZLE 1: BROADWAY MUSICALS

1. SOUND OF MUSIC
2. HELLO DOLLY
3. THE MUSIC MAN
4. OLIVER
5. GREASE
6. THE PRODUCERS
7. SHOWBOAT
8. A CHORUS LINE
9. WEST SIDE STORY
10. CHICAGO
11. PORGY AND BESS
12. HAIRSPRAY
13. THE WIZ
14. THE LION KING
15. OKLAHOMA
16. FUNNY GIRL
17. SOUTH PACIFIC
18. WICKED
19. KISS ME KATE
20. EVITA
21. LES MISERABLES
22. ANNIE
23. CABARET
24. AVENUE Q

PUZZLE 2: CLASSICAL COMPOSERS

#	Composer	Code	First name
1	BACH	N	Johann Sebastian
2	DEBUSSY	D	Claude
3	BRAHMS	O	Johannes
4	PROKOFIEV	V	Sergei
5	WAGNER	S / T	Richard
6	LISZT	G	Franz
7	MENDELSSOHN	F	Felix
8	GRIEG	E	Edvard
9	MOZART	W	Wolfgang Amadeus
10	SAINT SAENS	C	Camille
11	MAHLER	L	Gustav
12	CHOPIN	H	Frederic
13	BRUCKNER	A	Anton
14	RAVEL	Q	Maurice
15	BIZET	J	Georges
16	TCHAIKOVSKY	R	Peter Ilyich
17	BARTOK	B	Bela
18	BERLIOZ	M	Hector
19	VERDI	K	Guiseppi
20	RACHMANINOV	U	Serge
21	STRAUSS	S / T	Richard
22	BEETHOVEN	P	Ludwig Van
23	HANDEL	I	George Frideric

PUZZLE 3: MUSICAL INSTRUMENTS

#	Instrument	Code	Family
1	TIMPANI	P	Percussion
2	SOUSAPHONE	B	Brass
3	BASSOON	W	Woodwinds
4	TUBA	B	Brass
5	UKELELE	S	Strings
6	CLARINET	W	Woodwinds
7	PIANO	S	Strings
8	VIOLIN	S	Strings
9	SNARE DRUM	P	Percussion
10	GLOCKENSPIEL	P	Percussion
11	PICCOLO	W	Woodwinds
12	FLUTE	W	Woodwinds
13	XYLOPHONE	P	Percussion
14	FRENCH HORN	B	Brass
15	BANJO	S	Strings
16	ZITHER	S	Strings
17	TAMBOURINE	P	Percussion
18	CELLO	S	Strings
19	GUITAR	S	Strings
20	SAXOPHONE	W	Woodwinds
21	TRUMPET	B	Brass
22	CYMBALS	P	Percussion
23	TROMBONE	B	Brass
24	MARACAS	P	Percussion

NOTE: Line 3 is also correct as "BASS" - Strings

PUZZLE 4: MUSICAL GENRES

1 | P | S | A | L | M | O | R | A | T | O | R | I | O
2 | | | | E | T | U | D | E
3 | | | M | A | R | C | H
4 | | C | H | O | R | A | L | E
5 | | | P | R | E | L | U | D | E
6 | | | | R | H | A | P | S | O | D | Y
7 | | S | E | R | E | N | A | D | E
8 | | | | F | A | N | F | A | R | E
9 | | | | | M | O | T | E | T
10 | | | | | S | Y | M | P | H | O | N | Y
11 | | | | | F | U | G | U | E
12 | R | O | U | N | D | | W | A | L | T | Z
13 | | O | P | E | R | E | T | T | A
14 | | | | | M | I | N | U | E | T
15 | A | N | T | H | E | M
16 | | | | | | S | O | N | A | T | A
17 | H | Y | M | N | C | A | N | T | A | T | A
18 | | | J | A | Z | Z | O | C | T | E | T
19 | | | | | | B | L | U | E | S
20 | | | C | O | N | C | E | R | T | O
21 | | | | | N | O | C | T | U | R | N | E
22 | | | R | O | C | K | | C | A | N | O | N
23 | | | | | J | I | V | E
24 | A | R | I | A | | O | V | E | R | T | U | R | E

PUZZLE 5: MUSICAL TERMS

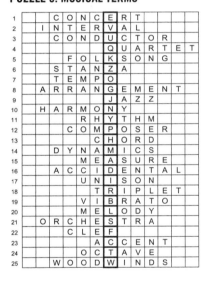
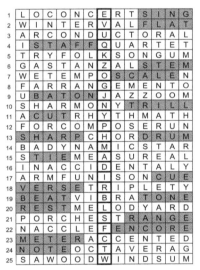

PUZZLE 6: ITALIAN MUSICAL TERMS

1 | | | | | | F | O | R | T | E
2 | | | E | S | P | R | E | S | S | I | V | O
3 | | | | F | E | R | M | A | T | A
4 | | | P | I | A | N | I | S | S | I | M | O
5 | | | S | F | O | R | Z | A | N | D | O
6 | M | A | R | C | A | T | O
7 | | | C | R | E | S | C | E | N | D | O
8 | | | L | E | G | A | T | O
9 | | | | V | I | V | A | C | E
10 | | D | I | M | I | N | U | E | N | D | O
11 | | | L | A | R | G | O
12 | | R | I | T | A | R | D | A | N | D | O
13 | | | M | A | E | S | T | O | S | O
14 | | | | A | N | D | A | N | T | E
15 | A | C | C | E | L | E | R | A | N | D | O
16 | | | T | R | A | N | Q | U | I | L | L | O
17 | | | | D | O | L | C | E
18 | S | T | A | C | C | A | T | O
19 | | | | | | P | R | E | S | T | O

G	Loud
M	Expressively
C	Hold; pause
Q	Very soft
H	Sudden strong accent
A	Emphasized, accented
I	Gradually louder
L	Smooth, connected
D	Lively
N	Gradually softer
B	Slow tempo
P	Gradually slower
F	Majestically
K	Walking tempo
S	Gradually faster
O	Quietly; calmly
R	Sweetly
J	Detached sounds
E	Very fast

PUZZLE 7: COMPOSERS

1	Georges Bizet	I	Carmen
2	George Frideric Handel	L	Messiah, Water Music
3	Ludwig van Beethoven	O	Für Elise, Moonlight Sonata
4	Peter Ilyich Tchaikovsky	K	1812 Overture, The Nutcracker
5	Claude Debussy	A	Clair de Lune, La Mer
6	Johann Sebastian Bach	J	Brandenburg Concertos, B-Minor Mass
7	Maurice Ravel	N	Bolero
8	Johannes Brahms	M	German Requiem, Liebeslieder Waltzes
9	Gustav Holst	E	The Planets
10	Antonin Dvorák	D	New World Symphony
11	Giuseppi Verdi	F	Aida
12	Jean Sibelius	H	Finlandia
13	Wolfgang Amadeus Mozart	B	Eine Kleine Nachtmusik, Don Giovanni
14	Franz Joseph Haydn	G	Surprise Symphony
15	Antonio Vivaldi	C	The Four Seasons

PUZZLE 8: CONTEMPORARY BROADWAY

1	Magic To Do	H	Pippin
2	Dancing Through Life	R	Wicked
3	The Circle of Life	O	The Lion King
4	One	A	A Chorus Line
5	You Can't Stop the Beat	T	Hairspray
6	Greased Lightnin'	E	Grease
7	Popular	R	Wicked
8	Be Our Guest	N	Beauty and the Beast
9	Memory	G	Cats
10	Hakuna Matata	O	The Lion King
11	The Music of the Night	S	Phantom of the Opera
12	Good Morning Baltimore	T	Hairspray
13	For Good	R	Wicked
14	What I Did For Love	A	A Chorus Line
15	Welcome to the 60's	T	Hairspray
16	Seasons of Love	I	Rent
17	We Go Together	E	Grease
18	The Winner Takes It All	C	Mamma Mia

G R E A T O R C H E S T R A T I O N
9 13 17 4 12 10 7 18 1 6 11 15 2 14 5 16 3 8

PUZZLE 9: CLASSIC BROADWAY

1	Tonight	W	West Side Story
2	I Could Have Danced All Night	Y	My Fair Lady
3	My Favorite Things	A	The Sound of Music
4	Tomorrow	N	Annie
5	Food, Glorious Food	O	Oliver
6	People	U	Funny Girl
7	Some Enchanted Evening	C	South Pacific
8	If I Were a Rich Man	R	Fiddler on the Roof
9	Somewhere	W	West Side Story
10	Do-Re-Mi	A	The Sound of Music
11	Summertime	B	Porgy and Bess
12	The Impossible Dream	L	The Man of La Mancha
13	On the Street Where You Live	Y	My Fair Lady
14	Getting to Know You	I	The King and I
15	Tradition	R	Fiddler on the Roof
16	Climb Every Mountain	A	The Sound of Music
17	Consider Yourself	O	Oliver
18	Ol' Man River	S	Showboat
19	Seventy-Six Trombones	M	The Music Man
20	Oh, What a Beautiful Morning	K	Oklahoma
21	Luck Be a Lady	E	Guys and Dolls
22	I'm a Yankee Doodle Dandy	D	George M

N E W Y O R K B R O A D W A Y M U S I C A L
4 21 9 2 17 8 20 11 15 5 10 22 1 16 13 19 6 18 14 7 3 12

PUZZLE 10: CHRISTMAS CAROLS

F	1.	O Come, All Ye Faithful
H	2.	We Three Kings
G	3.	Away in a Manger
J	4.	What Child Is This?
A	5.	Joy to the World
B	6.	O Little Town of Bethlehem
I	7.	The First Noel
C	8.	Silent Night
E	9.	Hark! The Herald Angels Sing
D	10.	Angels We Have Heard on High

PUZZLE 11: CHRISTMAS SONGS

F	1.	Jingle Bells
H	2.	We Wish You a Merry Christmas
E	3.	Deck the Hall
J	4.	Carol of the Bells
G	5.	The Twelve Days of Christmas
I	6.	Here We Come A-Caroling
B	7.	The Holly and the Ivy
C	8.	Good King Wenceslas
D	9.	Up on the Housetop
A	10.	Jolly Old St. Nicholas

PUZZLE 12: CHILDHOOD SONGS

C	1.	London Bridge Is Falling Down
E	2.	I've Been Working on the Railroad
A	3.	Three Blind Mice
D	4.	Mary Had a Little Lamb
G	5.	Rock-A-Bye Baby
J	6.	Row, Row, Row Your Boat
B	7.	Twinkle, Twinkle Little Star
I	8.	The Isty-Bitsy Spider
F	9.	Ring Around the Rosie
H	10.	Old MadDonald Had a Farm

PUZZLE 13: CAMP SONGS

H	1.	Kum Ba Yah
J	2.	If You're Happy and You Know It
C	3.	Head, Shoulders, Knees and Toes
F	4.	This Old Man
I	5.	Found a Peanut/Clementine
B	6.	Bingo
A	7.	Frère Jacques
E	8.	In a Cabin in the Wood
G	9.	Take Me Out to the Ball Game
D	10.	Michael Finnigan

SECTION 4 - MUSICAL SUDOKU

PUZZLE 14: MUSIC NOTE

U	E	I	O	C	M	S	N	T
N	C	S	T	I	E	M	U	O
T	M	O	U	N	S	C	I	E
S	I	U	M	O	N	T	E	C
M	O	E	I	T	C	N	S	U
C	N	T	S	E	U	I	O	M
I	S	M	E	U	T	O	C	N
O	U	C	N	M	I	E	T	S
E	T	N	C	S	O	U	M	I

PUZZLE 15: MUSIC NOTE

C	M	O	I	T	E	U	N	S
I	U	N	C	S	O	M	E	T
S	T	E	U	M	N	I	C	O
O	N	M	E	U	S	T	I	C
E	I	S	M	C	T	O	U	N
U	C	T	N	O	I	E	S	M
M	S	I	O	N	U	C	T	E
T	E	C	S	I	M	N	O	U
N	O	U	T	E	C	S	M	I

PUZZLE 16: MUSIC NOTE

N	M	E	T	I	S	O	U	C
U	C	I	E	O	N	M	S	T
O	T	S	U	M	C	N	I	E
M	I	N	C	U	E	S	T	O
C	S	T	M	N	O	U	E	I
E	U	O	S	T	I	C	N	M
I	N	M	O	E	U	T	C	S
S	O	U	I	C	T	E	M	N
T	E	C	N	S	M	I	O	U

PUZZLE 17: MUSIC NOTE

E	O	T	S	U	I	C	N	M
C	N	U	M	O	E	S	I	T
M	I	S	T	C	N	E	U	O
N	S	E	C	I	T	O	M	U
O	M	C	E	N	U	I	T	S
U	T	I	O	S	M	N	E	C
I	U	O	N	M	C	T	S	E
T	C	N	U	E	S	M	O	I
S	E	M	I	T	O	U	C	N

PUZZLE 18: TRIANGLES

T	L	G	S	A	R	E	N	I
I	N	S	T	E	L	R	G	A
A	R	E	I	N	G	T	S	L
L	G	N	R	I	S	A	T	E
S	E	I	N	T	A	L	R	G
R	T	A	G	L	E	S	I	N
E	I	R	A	G	T	N	L	S
N	S	L	E	R	I	G	A	T
G	A	T	L	S	N	I	E	R

PUZZLE 19: TRIANGLES

S	T	A	E	N	L	R	I	G
G	I	N	A	R	T	S	L	E
E	L	R	G	S	I	A	N	T
A	S	T	R	I	N	E	G	L
R	N	E	L	A	G	I	T	S
I	G	L	T	E	S	N	A	R
T	R	S	N	L	A	G	E	I
N	E	G	I	T	R	L	S	A
L	A	I	S	G	E	T	R	N

PUZZLE 20: TRIANGLES

L	E	A	G	N	S	R	T	I
G	R	N	T	A	I	L	S	E
S	T	I	L	R	E	A	N	G
T	A	R	N	G	L	I	E	S
N	G	E	I	S	A	T	L	R
I	S	L	E	T	R	G	A	N
E	N	T	R	L	G	S	I	A
A	L	G	S	I	N	E	R	T
R	I	S	A	E	T	N	G	L

PUZZLE 21: TRIANGLES

T	S	N	L	R	E	I	G	A
I	G	L	A	N	S	R	E	T
E	R	A	G	I	T	N	L	S
L	E	R	S	G	A	T	I	N
N	I	S	R	T	L	E	A	G
A	T	G	N	E	I	L	S	R
G	N	I	E	A	R	S	T	L
R	L	T	I	S	G	A	N	E
S	A	E	T	L	N	G	R	I

PUZZLE 22: C MAJOR KEY

M	K	Y	C	A	E	J	O	R
A	E	R	K	J	O	C	Y	M
C	J	O	M	Y	R	E	K	A
J	A	M	R	O	K	Y	C	E
K	O	C	Y	E	M	A	R	J
Y	R	E	A	C	J	K	M	O
O	Y	A	J	M	C	R	E	K
R	M	J	E	K	Y	O	A	C
E	C	K	O	R	A	M	J	Y

PUZZLE 23: C MAJOR KEY

E	K	O	R	Y	J	M	C	A
Y	J	C	O	M	A	R	K	E
A	M	R	E	C	K	Y	O	J
C	A	J	K	E	M	O	Y	R
R	Y	K	J	A	O	E	M	C
M	O	E	Y	R	C	A	J	K
K	E	Y	C	O	R	J	A	M
O	C	A	M	J	E	K	R	Y
J	R	M	A	K	Y	C	E	O

PUZZLE 24: C MAJOR KEY

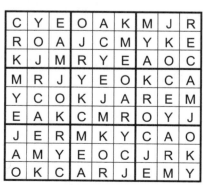

C	Y	E	O	A	K	M	J	R
R	O	A	J	C	M	Y	K	E
K	J	M	R	Y	E	A	O	C
M	R	J	Y	E	O	K	C	A
Y	C	O	K	J	A	R	E	M
E	A	K	C	M	R	O	Y	J
J	E	R	M	K	Y	C	A	O
A	M	Y	E	O	C	J	R	K
O	K	C	A	R	J	E	M	Y

PUZZLE 25: C MAJOR KEY

R	A	K	M	E	Y	O	J	C
Y	M	J	O	C	R	E	K	A
O	C	E	A	K	J	Y	M	R
A	E	Y	C	O	M	K	R	J
K	R	C	J	Y	E	A	O	M
M	J	O	K	R	A	C	Y	E
C	O	A	R	M	K	J	E	Y
J	Y	R	E	A	O	M	C	K
E	K	M	Y	J	C	R	A	O

PUZZLE 26: A MINOR KEY

O	R	Y	N	M	K	I	E	A
M	I	E	A	R	O	N	K	Y
K	N	A	Y	E	I	O	M	R
I	E	N	R	K	M	Y	A	O
R	Y	K	E	O	A	M	N	I
A	O	M	I	Y	N	E	R	K
Y	K	I	M	A	E	R	O	N
N	M	O	K	I	R	A	Y	E
E	A	R	O	N	Y	K	I	M

PUZZLE 27: A MINOR KEY

M	A	I	K	E	N	O	R	Y
K	R	Y	A	O	M	I	N	E
O	N	E	Y	R	I	A	K	M
Y	M	K	E	A	O	N	I	R
I	E	R	N	M	K	Y	O	A
N	O	A	I	Y	R	E	M	K
E	I	M	O	K	A	R	Y	N
R	Y	N	M	I	E	K	A	O
A	K	O	R	N	Y	M	E	I

PUZZLE 28: A MINOR KEY

E	A	Y	N	K	I	R	O	M
R	I	K	O	E	M	A	Y	N
M	O	N	R	A	Y	E	I	K
I	R	O	K	M	A	N	E	Y
Y	N	A	E	R	O	K	M	I
K	E	M	Y	I	N	O	R	A
O	M	I	A	N	E	Y	K	R
A	Y	R	M	O	K	I	N	E
N	K	E	I	Y	R	M	A	O

PUZZLE 29: A MINOR KEY

K	N	Y	A	E	I	M	R	O
R	E	O	K	N	M	Y	I	A
M	A	I	O	Y	R	E	N	K
O	M	K	R	I	N	A	Y	E
N	Y	A	M	O	E	R	K	I
E	I	R	Y	A	K	O	M	N
I	R	N	E	M	O	K	A	Y
Y	K	E	N	R	A	I	O	M
A	O	M	I	K	Y	N	E	R

PUZZLE 30: SIGNATURE

N	I	U	A	E	T	S	R	G
R	E	S	G	I	U	N	T	A
A	T	G	S	N	R	U	E	I
U	A	R	I	T	N	G	S	E
E	G	I	U	A	S	R	N	T
T	S	N	E	R	G	A	I	U
S	U	E	R	G	I	T	A	N
G	N	A	T	S	E	I	U	R
I	R	T	N	U	A	E	G	S

PUZZLE 31: SIGNATURE

T	E	N	R	G	I	U	A	S
S	R	U	N	T	A	E	I	G
A	G	I	S	U	E	T	N	R
R	A	S	T	E	G	I	U	N
N	I	E	U	S	R	G	T	A
U	T	G	I	A	N	R	S	E
G	U	R	A	N	T	S	E	I
E	S	A	G	I	U	N	R	T
I	N	T	E	R	S	A	G	U

PUZZLE 32: SIGNATURE

G	A	T	U	E	R	S	N	I
U	R	E	I	S	N	T	A	G
S	I	N	G	T	A	R	E	U
N	G	I	R	U	S	A	T	E
E	T	A	N	G	I	U	R	S
R	S	U	E	A	T	G	I	N
T	N	S	A	I	G	E	U	R
A	U	R	S	N	E	I	G	T
I	E	G	T	R	U	N	S	A

PUZZLE 33: SIGNATURE

G	E	T	S	R	U	N	A	I
I	R	U	N	A	G	T	E	S
A	S	N	E	I	T	R	U	G
U	I	G	A	E	R	S	T	N
T	A	S	U	N	I	E	G	R
R	N	E	G	T	S	A	I	U
S	G	A	T	U	N	I	R	E
E	U	R	I	S	A	G	N	T
N	T	I	R	G	E	U	S	A

PUZZLE 34: INTERVALS

N	V	I	A	R	L	E	S	T
R	S	A	I	T	E	V	L	N
T	E	L	S	N	V	A	I	R
L	I	E	T	A	R	S	N	V
V	R	T	N	L	S	I	E	A
S	A	N	V	E	I	R	T	L
I	L	R	E	V	N	T	A	S
A	N	S	R	I	T	L	V	E
E	T	V	L	S	A	N	R	I

PUZZLE 35: INTERVALS

E	S	R	T	I	N	L	A	V
L	T	N	A	V	S	R	E	I
A	V	I	R	E	L	S	T	N
V	E	S	I	T	A	N	L	R
T	R	A	L	N	V	E	I	S
N	I	L	E	S	R	A	V	T
R	A	V	S	L	I	T	N	E
I	L	T	N	R	E	V	S	A
S	N	E	V	A	T	I	R	L

PUZZLE 36: INTERVALS

A	R	T	I	E	N	S	L	V
V	I	N	L	T	S	E	A	R
L	S	E	R	V	A	T	I	N
S	E	I	A	N	R	V	T	L
T	N	A	V	S	L	I	R	E
R	L	V	E	I	T	A	N	S
E	A	R	S	L	I	N	V	T
I	T	S	N	R	V	L	E	A
N	V	L	T	A	E	R	S	I

PUZZLE 37: INTERVALS

I	N	A	R	S	E	T	V	L
L	R	V	T	I	A	S	E	N
T	E	S	V	N	L	R	A	I
S	I	E	L	T	R	V	N	A
N	T	L	A	V	I	E	R	S
A	V	R	N	E	S	I	L	T
V	A	I	S	R	N	L	T	E
R	S	N	E	L	T	A	I	V
E	L	T	I	A	V	N	S	R

PUZZLE 38: CLARINETS

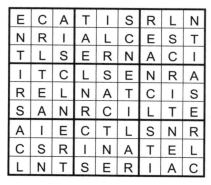

E	C	A	T	I	S	R	L	N
N	R	I	A	L	C	E	S	T
T	L	S	E	R	N	A	C	I
I	T	C	L	S	E	N	R	A
R	E	L	N	A	T	C	I	S
S	A	N	R	C	I	L	T	E
A	I	E	C	T	L	S	N	R
C	S	R	I	N	A	T	E	L
L	N	T	S	E	R	I	A	C

PUZZLE 39: CLARINETS

T	I	S	R	N	C	L	A	E
L	E	C	T	I	A	S	R	N
A	R	N	S	E	L	T	C	I
N	T	R	E	L	S	A	I	C
C	A	E	N	T	I	R	S	L
S	L	I	A	C	R	N	E	T
E	S	L	C	R	N	I	T	A
I	C	A	L	S	T	E	N	R
R	N	T	I	A	E	C	L	S

PUZZLE 40: CLARINETS

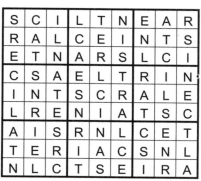

S	C	I	L	T	N	E	A	R
R	A	L	C	E	I	N	T	S
E	T	N	A	R	S	L	C	I
C	S	A	E	L	T	R	I	N
I	N	T	S	C	R	A	L	E
L	R	E	N	I	A	T	S	C
A	I	S	R	N	L	C	E	T
T	E	R	I	A	C	S	N	L
N	L	C	T	S	E	I	R	A

PUZZLE 41: CLARINETS

L	C	S	T	A	I	R	E	N
E	T	R	N	S	C	A	I	L
I	A	N	L	E	R	C	S	T
A	L	C	I	R	E	N	T	S
N	S	I	C	L	T	E	R	A
R	E	T	A	N	S	L	C	I
C	R	A	S	T	N	I	L	E
S	I	L	E	C	A	T	N	R
T	N	E	R	I	L	S	A	C

PUZZLE 42: BARITONES

S	B	R	A	E	N	T	I	O
T	A	N	I	R	O	B	E	S
O	E	I	S	B	T	N	A	R
I	N	S	R	A	B	E	O	T
B	T	E	O	N	S	A	R	I
R	O	A	T	I	E	S	B	N
N	R	T	E	O	A	I	S	B
E	S	O	B	T	I	R	N	A
A	I	B	N	S	R	O	T	E

PUZZLE 43: BARITONES

E	I	B	R	O	T	A	N	S
N	T	S	B	A	E	R	O	I
R	A	O	N	I	S	B	E	T
S	O	T	I	R	A	E	B	N
A	N	E	T	B	O	I	S	R
I	B	R	E	S	N	O	T	A
T	S	A	O	E	I	N	R	B
B	E	I	S	N	R	T	A	O
O	R	N	A	T	B	S	I	E

PUZZLE 44: BARITONES

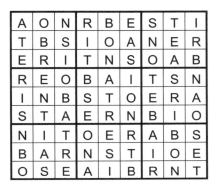

A	O	N	R	B	E	S	T	I
T	B	S	I	O	A	N	E	R
E	R	I	T	N	S	O	A	B
R	E	O	B	A	I	T	S	N
I	N	B	S	T	O	E	R	A
S	T	A	E	R	N	B	I	O
N	I	T	O	E	R	A	B	S
B	A	R	N	S	T	I	O	E
O	S	E	A	I	B	R	N	T

PUZZLE 45: BARITONES

R	A	S	N	B	T	I	E	O
O	N	I	A	E	R	S	T	B
B	E	T	S	O	I	A	N	R
A	T	E	I	N	B	O	R	S
S	I	R	O	A	E	N	B	T
N	O	B	R	T	S	E	A	I
E	R	O	B	I	N	T	S	A
T	B	A	E	S	O	R	I	N
I	S	N	T	R	A	B	O	E

PUZZLE 46: DYNAMICS

mp	sfz	p	f	>	<	ff	pp	mf
f	mf	ff	p	pp	sfz	<	mp	>
>	pp	<	mf	ff	mp	sfz	f	p
<	mp	>	pp	p	f	mf	ff	sfz
mf	p	f	ff	sfz	>	mp	<	pp
sfz	ff	pp	mp	<	mf	p	>	f
pp	<	mf	>	mp	p	f	sfz	ff
ff	f	sfz	<	mf	pp	>	p	mp
p	>	mp	sfz	f	ff	pp	mf	<

PUZZLE 47: DYNAMICS

sfz	mf	p	pp	f	<	ff	>	mp
ff	mp	f	p	sfz	>	pp	mf	<
pp	>	<	mf	ff	mp	p	sfz	f
mf	pp	ff	mp	<	p	>	f	sfz
f	<	sfz	ff	>	mf	mp	pp	p
mp	p	>	f	pp	sfz	<	ff	mf
p	sfz	mp	>	mf	pp	f	<	ff
<	f	pp	sfz	p	ff	mf	mp	>
>	ff	mf	<	mp	f	sfz	p	pp

PUZZLE 48: DYNAMICS

mf	f	<	ff	pp	sfz	mp	p	>
p	ff	mp	f	mf	>	sfz	pp	<
pp	>	sfz	<	mp	p	ff	f	mf
>	pp	f	mf	p	mp	<	sfz	ff
ff	mp	p	sfz	<	f	>	mf	pp
<	sfz	mf	pp	>	ff	p	mp	f
sfz	mf	pp	mp	ff	<	f	>	p
mp	p	ff	>	f	mf	pp	<	sfz
f	<	>	p	sfz	pp	mf	ff	mp

PUZZLE 49: DYNAMICS

<	f	mp	>	pp	sfz	ff	mf	p
ff	sfz	p	<	mp	mf	f	>	pp
pp	>	mf	ff	p	f	<	mp	sfz
f	mp	sfz	pp	ff	>	p	<	mf
p	ff	<	sfz	mf	mp	pp	f	>
>	mf	pp	p	f	<	mp	sfz	ff
mp	p	>	f	sfz	ff	mf	pp	<
sfz	pp	f	mf	<	p	>	ff	mp
mf	<	ff	mp	>	pp	sfz	p	f

PUZZLE 50: MUSICAL SCALE

♭	B	G	C	F	#	E	D	A
A	E	C	G	D	B	♭	F	#
#	D	F	A	♭	E	G	B	C
G	F	#	D	E	C	B	A	♭
E	♭	B	#	G	A	D	C	F
C	A	D	F	B	♭	#	G	E
B	G	♭	E	C	F	A	#	D
D	C	A	♭	#	G	F	E	B
F	#	E	B	A	D	C	♭	G

PUZZLE 51: MUSICAL SCALE

C	B	D	F	E	#	G	♭	A
A	♭	#	B	D	C	F	E	G
E	F	G	#	A	♭	C	B	D
G	D	♭	E	#	C	A	F	B
#	A	F	♭	B	D	E	G	C
B	E	C	G	#	♭	F	D	A
F	C	E	D	♭	G	B	#	A
D	#	B	A	♭	E	G	C	F
♭	G	A	C	F	#	B	D	E

PUZZLE 52: MUSICAL SCALE

G	E	#	D	♭	F	C	A	B
F	B	A	G	C	#	D	E	♭
D	C	♭	A	B	E	F	G	#
♭	F	C	B	G	D	E	#	A
B	#	E	F	A	♭	G	D	C
A	D	G	E	#	C	B	♭	F
E	A	D	♭	F	B	#	C	G
C	G	B	#	E	A	♭	F	D
#	♭	F	C	D	G	A	B	E

PUZZLE 53: MUSICAL SCALE

A	#	D	G	C	♭	E	F	B
E	G	F	A	♭	B	D	#	C
C	B	♭	#	F	E	A	D	G
♭	D	E	F	#	G	B	A	C
G	A	B	E	#	D	♭	C	F
F	C	#	♭	A	B	G	E	D
B	E	G	C	♭	#	F	D	A
D	F	A	B	E	#	♭	C	G
#	♭	C	D	G	A	F	B	E

PUZZLE 54: MUSICAL SYMBOLS

PUZZLE 55: MUSICAL SYMBOLS

PUZZLE 56: MUSICAL SYMBOLS

PUZZLE 57: MUSICAL SYMBOLS

PUZZLE 58: TREBLE CLEFF CROSSWORD 1

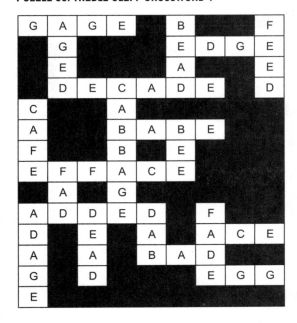

PUZZLE 59: TREBLE CLEFF CROSSWORD 2

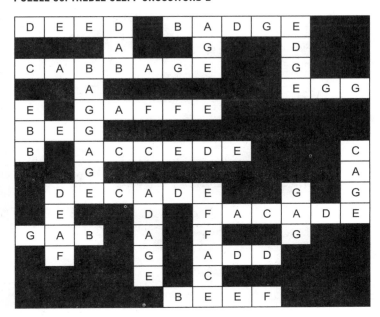

PUZZLE 60: BASS CLEFF CROSSWORD 1

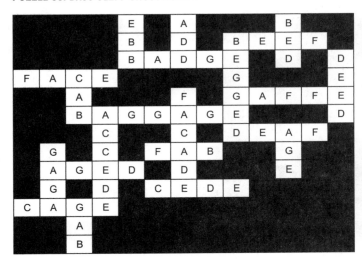

PUZZLE 61: BASS CLEFF CROSSWORD 2

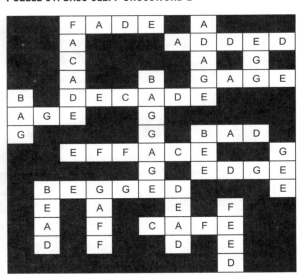

PUZZLE 62: CONTEMPORARY BROADWAY

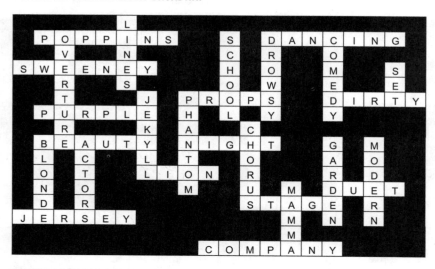

PUZZLE 63: CLASSIC BROADWAY

PUZZLE 64: BROADWAY MUSICALS

1. Z H E M → **C A T S**

2. T D N E H → **E V I T A**

3. E C T | M A F X B | A G | U F M N Z → **T H E** | **S O U N D** | **O F** | **M U S I C**

4. U Q | G H N S | J H B Q → **M Y** | **F A I R** | **L A D Y**

5. E C T | Y N X R | H X B | N → **T H E** | **K I N G** | **A N D** | **I**

6. I N Z Y T B → **W I C K E D**

7. R F Q M | H X B | B A J J M → **G U Y S** | **A N D** | **D O L L S**

8. C H N S M K S H Q → **H A I R S P R A Y**

9. U H U U H | U N H → **M A M M A** | **M I A**

10. H X X N T → **A N N I E**

11. H | Z C A S F M | J N X T → **A** | **C H O R U S** | **L I N E**

12. E C T | U F M N Z | U H X → **T H E** | **M U S I C** | **M A N**

PUZZLE 65: CHRISTMAS SONGS

1. R J U Q F Z | K F U U R → **S I L V E R** | **B E L L S**

2. V F Z F | B C H F R | R X G M X | B U X E R → **H E R E** | **C O M E S** | **S A N T A** | **C L A U S**

3. E O | C G | M V F | V C E R F M C O → **U P** | **O N** | **T H E** | **H O U S E T O P**

4. A F B I | M V F | V X U U → **D E C K** | **T H E** | **H A L L**

5. W J G D U F | K F U U R → **J I N G L E** | **B E L L S**

6. U F M | J M | R G C L → **L E T** | **I T** | **S N O W**

7. L V J M F | B V Z J R M H X R → **W H I T E** | **C H R I S T M A S**

8. R U F J D V | Z J A F → **S L E I G H** | **R I D E**

9. S Z C R M P | M V F | R G C L H X G → **F R O S T Y** | **T H E** | **S N O W M A N**

PUZZLE 66: CHRISTMAS CAROLS

1. `Q X Q F | U E | Q | Y Q E T K K`
   A W A Y   I N   A   M A N G E R

2. `O N K | G U H C O | E S K R`
   T H E   F I R S T   N O E L

3. `X N Q O | W N U R J | U C | O N U C`
   W H A T   C H I L D   I S   T H I S

4. `S | N S R F | E U T N O`
   O   H O L Y   N I G H T

5. `B S F | O S | O N K | X S H R J`
   J O Y   T O   T H E   W O R L D

6. `X K | O N H K K | P U E T C`
   W E   T H R E E   K I N G S

7. `R U O O R K | J H A Y Y K H | I S F`
   L I T T L E   D R U M M E R   B O Y

8. `S | W S Y K | Q R R | F K | G Q U O N G A R`
   O   C O M E   A L L   Y E   F A I T H F U L

9. `C U R K E O | E U T N O`
   S I L E N T   N I G H T

PUZZLE 67: CLASSICAL COMPOSERS

1. `C J F R X X | T Z Q R T V H R X | Q R E F`
   J O H A N N   S E B A S T I A N   B A C H

2. `G O Z N Z O H E | E F J L H X`
   F R E D E R I C   C H O P I N

3. `M Z J O M Z | G O H N Z O H E | F R X N Z D`
   G E O R G E   F R I D E R I C   H A N D E L

4. `M P T V R I | U R F D Z O`
   G U S T A V   M A H L E R

5. `D P N S H M | I R X | Q Z Z V F J I Z X`
   L U D W I G   V A N   B E E T H O V E N

6. `G O R X W | D H T W V`
   F R A N Z   L I S Z T

7. `E D R P N Z | N Z Q P T T K`
   C L A U D E   D E B U S S Y

8. `U R P O H E Z | O R I Z D`
   M A U R I C E   R A V E L

9. `R X V J X H J | I H I R D N H`
   A N T O N I O   V I V A L D I

10. `C J F R X X Z T | Q O R F U T`
    J O H A N N E S   B R A H M S

PUZZLE 68: MODERN COMPOSERS

1 N F E B T R | O O P D E | R T I I T B
   A N D R E W | L L O Y D | W E B B E R

2 J P O T | X P B G T B
   C O L E | P O R T E R

3 O T B P D | N F E T B A P F
   L E R O Y | A N D E R S O N

4 T O G P F | W P K F
   E L T O N | J O H N

5 U T P B U T | U T B A K R C F
   G E O R G E | G E R S H W I N

6 N N B P F | J P X O N F E
   A A R O N | C O P L A N D

7 K T F B D | L N F J C F C
   H E N R Y | M A N C I N I

8 W P K F | R C O O C N L A
   J O H N | W I L L I A M S

9 O T P F N B E | I T B F A G T C F
   L E O N A R D | B E R N S T E I N

10 W P K F | X K C O O C X | A P Q A N
   J O H N | P H I L L I P | S O U S A

PUZZLE 69: MUSICAL INSTRUMENTS

1 C Q L W K
   P I A N O

2 O U G X D
   F L U T E

3 K H K D
   O B O E

4 R L Y K C M K W D
   S A X O P H O N E

5 X J G T C D X
   T R U M P E T

6 E U L J Q W D X
   C L A R I N E T

7 V J G T R
   D R U M S

8 O J D W E M | M K J W
   F R E N C H | H O R N

9 N Q K U Q W
   V I O L I N

10 E D U U K
   C E L L O

11 X G H L
   T U B A

12 X J K T H K W D
   T R O M B O N E

PUZZLE 70: SONGS BY THE BEATLES

1. H Y C — U N A C H — W N M
   S H E _ L O V E S _ Y O U

2. S Q B F C S — S N — T Q G C
   T I C K E T _ T O _ R I D E

3. Y C U Z
   H E L P

4. W C U U N L — H M D K V T Q J C
   Y E L L O W _ S U B M A R I N E

5. W C H S C T G V W
   Y E S T E R D A Y

6. Y C W — X M G C
   H E Y _ J U D E

7. Z V Z C T D V B F — L T Q S C T
   P A P E R B A C K _ W R I T E R

8. V — Y V T G — G V W H — J Q R Y S
   A _ H A R D _ D A Y S _ N I G H T

9. R C S — D V B F
   G E T _ B A C K

PUZZLE 71: FAVORITE KIDS' SONGS

1. L N Y — M D T Z Y T — S J — L N Y — W Y P P
   T H E _ F A R M E R _ I N _ T H E _ D E L L

2. L N T Y Y — U P S J W — Z S E Y
   T H R E E _ B L I N D _ M I C E

3. Z D T K — N D W — D — P S L L P Y — P D Z U
   M A R Y _ H A D _ A _ L I T T L E _ L A M B

4. I F I — V F Y A — L N Y — O Y D A Y P
   P O P _ G O E S _ T H E _ W E A S E L

5. T F O — T F O — T F O — K F Q T — U F D L
   R O W _ R O W _ R O W _ Y O U R _ B O A T

6. K D J G Y Y — W F F W P Y
   Y A N K E E _ D O O D L E

7. L N Y — S L A K — U S L A K — A I S W Y T
   T H E _ I T S Y _ B I T S Y _ S P I D E R

8. N F G Y K — I F G Y K
   H O K E Y _ P O K E Y

9. S Z — D — P S L L P Y — L Y D I F L
   I M _ A _ L I T T L E _ T E A P O T

10. T S J V — D T F Q J W — L N Y — T F A S Y
    R I N G _ A R O U N D _ T H E _ R O S I E

PUZZLE 72: PATRIOTIC SONGS

1. | K | T | W | | Q | B | H | N | N | | I | Y | H | S | Z | A | I |
   |---|---|---|---|---|---|---|---|---|---|---|---|---|---|---|---|---|
   | G | O | D | | B | L | E | S | S | | A | M | E | R | I | C | A |

2. | Y | C | | A | T | J | P | R | S | C | | R | Z | N | | T | O | | R | V | H | H |
   |---|---|---|---|---|---|---|---|---|---|---|---|---|---|---|---|---|---|---|---|---|---|
   | M | Y | | C | O | U | N | T | R | Y | | T | I | S | | O | F | | T | H | E | E |

3. | C | T | J | S | H | | I | | K | S | I | P | W | | T | B | W | | O | B | I | K |
   |---|---|---|---|---|---|---|---|---|---|---|---|---|---|---|---|---|---|---|---|---|---|
   | Y | O | U | R | E | | A | | G | R | A | N | D | | O | L | D | | F | L | A | G |

4. | C | I | P | E | H | H | | W | T | T | W | B | H | | W | I | P | W | C |
   |---|---|---|---|---|---|---|---|---|---|---|---|---|---|---|---|---|---|---|
   | Y | A | N | K | E | E | | D | O | O | D | L | E | | D | A | N | D | Y |

5. | K | T | W | | Q | B | H | N | N | | R | V | H | | J | N | I |
   |---|---|---|---|---|---|---|---|---|---|---|---|---|---|---|---|---|
   | G | O | D | | B | L | E | S | S | | T | H | E | | U | S | A |

6. | R | V | Z | N | | Z | N | | Y | C | | A | T | J | P | R | S | C |
   |---|---|---|---|---|---|---|---|---|---|---|---|---|---|---|---|---|---|
   | T | H | I | S | | I | S | | M | Y | | C | O | U | N | T | R | Y |

7.	N	R	I	S		N	M	I	P	K	B	H	W		Q	I	P	P	H	S
S	T	A	R		S	P	A	N	G	L	E	D		B	A	N	N	E	R

8.	I	Y	H	S	Z	A	I		R	V	H		Q	H	I	J	R	Z	O	J	B
A	M	E	R	I	C	A		T	H	E		B	E	A	U	T	I	F	U	L

9. | R | V | Z | N | | B | I | P | W | | Z | N | | C | T | J | S | | B | I | P | W |
   |---|---|---|---|---|---|---|---|---|---|---|---|---|---|---|---|---|---|---|---|---|---|
   | T | H | I | S | | L | A | N | D | | I | S | | Y | O | U | R | | L | A | N | D |

PUZZLE 73: MUSICAL INSTRUMENTS

1. | 5 | 18 | 18 | 23 | | 15 | 17 | 18 | 6 | 2 |
   |---|----|----|----|---|----|----|----|---|---|
   | W | O | O | D | | B | L | O | C | K |

2. | 9 | 17 | 18 | 6 | 2 | 1 | 25 | 26 | 3 | 12 | 1 | 17 |
   |---|----|----|---|---|---|----|----|---|----|---|----|
   | G | L | O | C | K | E | N | S | P | I | E | L |

3. | 8 | 12 | 4 | 20 | 1 | 7 |
   |---|----|---|----|---|---|
   | Z | I | T | H | E | R |

4. | 16 | 17 | 19 | 4 | 1 |
   |----|----|----|---|---|
   | F | L | U | T | E |

5. | 26 | 10 | 24 | 18 | 3 | 20 | 18 | 25 | 1 |
   |----|----|----|----|---|----|----|----|---|
   | S | A | X | O | P | H | O | N | E |

6. | 6 | 14 | 11 | 15 | 10 | 17 | 26 |
   |---|----|----|----|----|----|----|
   | C | Y | M | B | A | L | S |

7. | 2 | 1 | 4 | 4 | 17 | 1 | | 23 | 7 | 19 | 11 |
   |---|---|---|---|----|---|---|----|---|----|----|
   | K | E | T | T | L | E | | D | R | U | M |

8. | 15 | 10 | 25 | 22 | 18 |
   |----|----|----|----|----|
   | B | A | N | J | O |

9. | 13 | 12 | 18 | 17 | 12 | 25 |
   |----|----|----|----|----|----|
   | V | I | O | L | I | N |

10. | 24 | 14 | 17 | 18 | 3 | 20 | 18 | 25 | 1 |
    |----|----|----|----|---|----|----|----|---|
    | X | Y | L | O | P | H | O | N | E |

PUZZLE 74: COMPOSERS

1 | 5 | 13 | 10 | 20 | 23 | 3 | 11 | 14 |
   | G | E | R | S | H | W | I | N |

2 | 1 | 9 | 16 | 10 | 6 | 2 |
   | D | V | O | R | A | K |

3 | 12 | 13 | 10 | 14 | 20 | 8 | 13 | 11 | 14 |
   | B | E | R | N | S | T | E | I | N |

4 | 7 | 16 | 19 | 6 | 10 | 8 |
   | M | O | Z | A | R | T |

5 | 20 | 16 | 14 | 1 | 23 | 13 | 11 | 7 |
   | S | O | N | D | H | E | I | M |

6 | 22 | 16 | 4 | 26 | 6 | 14 | 1 |
   | C | O | P | L | A | N | D |

7 | 8 | 22 | 23 | 6 | 11 | 2 | 16 | 9 | 20 | 2 | 15 |
   | T | C | H | A | I | K | O | V | S | K | Y |

8 | 21 | 16 | 4 | 26 | 11 | 14 |
   | J | O | P | L | I | N |

9 | 1 | 13 | 12 | 24 | 20 | 20 | 15 |
   | D | E | B | U | S | S | Y |

10 | 17 | 6 | 24 | 10 | 13 |
   | F | A | U | R | E |

PUZZLE 75: ITALIAN MUSICAL TERMS

1 | 17 | 22 | 24 | 19 | 19 | 18 | 25 | 23 | 15 |
   | G | L | I | S | S | A | N | D | O |

2 | 7 | 24 | 12 | 12 | 24 | 13 | 18 | 11 | 15 |
   | P | I | Z | Z | I | C | A | T | O |

3 | 9 | 3 | 5 | 2 | 18 | 11 | 18 |
   | F | E | R | M | A | T | A |

4 | 11 | 5 | 18 | 25 | 20 | 16 | 24 | 22 | 22 | 15 |
   | T | R | A | N | Q | U | I | L | L | O |

5 | 13 | 18 | 23 | 3 | 25 | 12 | 18 |
   | C | A | D | E | N | Z | A |

6 | 18 | 5 | 7 | 3 | 17 | 17 | 24 | 15 |
   | A | R | P | E | G | G | I | O |

7 | 19 | 9 | 15 | 5 | 12 | 18 | 25 | 23 | 15 |
   | S | F | O | R | Z | A | N | D | O |

8 | 18 | 13 | 18 | 7 | 7 | 3 | 22 | 22 | 18 |
   | A | C | A | P | P | E | L | L | A |

9 | 1 | 24 | 8 | 5 | 18 | 11 | 15 |
   | V | I | B | R | A | T | O |

10 | 2 | 18 | 3 | 19 | 11 | 5 | 15 |
   | M | A | E | S | T | R | O |

SECTION 7 - MUSICAL CODES

PUZZLE 76: OPERAS

1. | 4 | 20 | 10 | | 14 | 6 | 13 | 14 | 10 | 13 | | 15 | 2 | | 26 | 10 | 17 | 24 | 3 | 3 | 10 |
   | T | H | E | | B | A | R | B | E | R | | O | F | | S | E | V | I | L | L | E |

2. | 11 | 6 | 7 | 3 | 24 | 6 | 18 | 18 | 24 |
   | P | A | G | L | I | A | C | C | I |

3. | 3 | 6 | | 4 | 13 | 6 | 17 | 24 | 6 | 4 | 6 |
   | L | A | | T | R | A | V | I | A | T | A |

4. | 18 | 6 | 13 | 8 | 10 | 21 |
   | C | A | R | M | E | N |

5. | 22 | 15 | 21 | | 7 | 24 | 15 | 17 | 6 | 21 | 21 | 24 |
   | D | O | N | | G | I | O | V | A | N | N | I |

6. | 4 | 20 | 10 | | 8 | 6 | 7 | 24 | 18 | | 2 | 3 | 9 | 4 | 10 |
   | T | H | E | | M | A | G | I | C | | F | L | U | T | E |

7. | 4 | 20 | 10 | | 8 | 6 | 13 | 13 | 24 | 6 | 7 | 10 | | 15 | 2 | | 2 | 24 | 7 | 6 | 13 | 15 |
   | T | H | E | | M | A | R | R | I | A | G | E | | O | F | | F | I | G | A | R | O |

8. | 4 | 15 | 26 | 18 | 6 |
   | T | O | S | C | A |

9. | 13 | 24 | 7 | 15 | 3 | 10 | 4 | 4 | 15 |
   | R | I | G | O | L | E | T | T | O |

10. | 6 | 24 | 22 | 6 |
    | A | I | D | A |

SECTION 8 - SCRAMBLED WORDS

PUZZLE 77: BROADWAY MUSICALS

1. | C | A | B | A | R | E | T |
   | | 30 | | | 21 | 1 | |

2. | H | A | I | R | S | P | R | A | Y |
   | | 2 | | 27 | | | 33 | | |

3. | O | L | I | V | E | R |
   | 24 | 16 | | 35 | 3 | |

4. | C | H | I | C | A | G | O |
   | | | 5 | | | 32 | 17 |

5. | T | I | T | A | N | I | C |
   | 18 | 31 | | 8 | 25 | | |

6. | O | K | L | A | H | O | M | A |
   | | 4 | 22 | | 20 | | | |

7. | G | R | E | A | S | E |
   | 29 | | 15 | | | 36 |

8. | R | A | G | T | I | M | E |
   | 37 | | 7 | 19 | | 14 | |

9. | A | N | N | I | E |
   | 13 | 9 | 28 | | |

10. | P | I | P | P | I | N |
    | | 11 | | | 23 | 6 |

11. | W | I | C | K | E | D |
    | 34 | 12 | 26 | | 10 | |

BONUS WORDS

11. | T | H | E | | K | I | N | G | | A | N | D | | I |
    | 1 | 2 | 3 | | 4 | 5 | 6 | 7 | | 8 | 9 | 10 | | 11 |

12. | C | A | M | E | L | O | T |
    | 12 | 13 | 14 | 15 | 16 | 17 | 18 |

13. | T | H | E | | L | I | O | N | | K | I | N | G |
    | 19 | 20 | 21 | | 22 | 23 | 24 | 25 | | 26 | 27 | 28 | 29 |

14. | B | I | G | | R | I | V | E | R |
    | 30 | 31 | 32 | | 33 | 34 | 35 | 36 | 37 |

PUZZLE 78: MUSICAL INSTRUMENTS

1. S N A R E [ ] D R U M
   (10) (14) (20) (3)

2. S A X O P H O N E
   (2) (15) (28)

3. T R U M P E T
   (24) (6) (11) (1)

4. C L A R I N E T
   (17) (9) (22)

5. T I M P A N I
   (8) (25) (18) (21)

6. A C C O R D I A N
   (29) (7) (26) (12)

7. O R G A N
   (5) (19) (23) (13)

8. C Y M B A L S
   (4) (27) (16)

BONUS WORDS

11. T A M B O U R I N E
    (1) (2) (3) (4) (5) (6) (7) (8) (9) (10)

12. M A N D O L I N
    (11) (12) (13) (14) (15) (16) (17) (18)

13. G U I T A R
    (19) (20) (21) (22) (23) (24)

14. P I A N O
    (25) (26) (27) (28) (29)

PUZZLE 79: MUSICAL TERMS

1. C O M P O S E R
   (3) (16) (22) (13)

2. M E A S U R E
   (18) (6) (29)

3. E N C O R E
   (15) (8)

4. L A R G O
   (31) (20) (1)

5. E T U D E
   (28) (7) (11)

6. L E G A T O
   (32) (21) (9) (27)

7. T E M P O
   (5) (10) (19)

8. V I B R A T O
   (30) (25) (2) (14)

9. B A T O N
   (12) (24) (26)

10. R H Y T H M
    (4) (23) (17)

BONUS WORDS

11. O R C H E S T R A
    (1) (2) (3) (4) (5) (6) (7) (8) (9)

12. M E T R O N O M E
    (10) (11) (12) (13) (14) (15) (16) (17) (18)

13. P R E S T O
    (19) (20) (21) (22) (23) (24)

14. I N T E R V A L
    (25) (26) (27) (28) (29) (30) (31) (32)

PUZZLE 80: MUSICAL TERMS

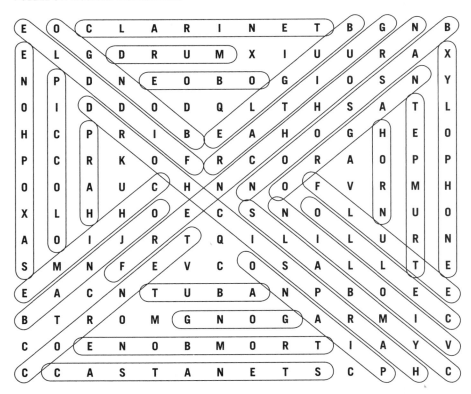

```
C  M  Y  E  N  R  U  T  C  O  N  A  C  B
O  M  H  D  I  T  E  N  O  R  L  H  A  P
N  A  E  T  O  N  I  J  V  T  O  T  E  B
D  E  R  T  Y  L  S  B  O  R  O  R  E  T
U  S  L  E  R  H  E  T  D  N  C  A  A  O
C  P  S  A  P  O  R  M  R  U  T  L  X  O
T  R  O  B  C  O  F  C  S  U  F  D  O  P
O  A  N  S  P  S  O  S  V  C  M  Z  J  M
R  H  G  I  H  M  I  E  G  O  H  E  M  E
H  S  A  C  P  O  V  N  C  M  L  O  N  T
U  N  R  O  N  A  I  I  C  S  E  U  I  T
O  A  S  H  T  R  S  S  V  O  S  T  M  R
M  E  V  C  T  U  N  O  T  E  D  A  E  E
R  N  O  S  M  S  C  O  R  E  R  A  B  R
```

PUZZLE 81: MUSICAL INSTRUMENTS

```
E  O  C  L  A  R  I  N  E  T  B  G  N  B
E  L  G  D  R  U  M  X  I  U  U  R  A  X
N  P  D  N  E  O  B  O  G  I  O  S  N  Y
O  I  C  D  D  O  D  Q  L  T  H  S  A  L
H  C  P  R  I  B  E  A  H  O  G  H  T  O
P  C  R  K  O  F  R  C  O  R  A  O  E  P
O  O  R  A  U  C  H  N  N  O  F  V  R  H
X  L  A  H  O  E  C  S  N  O  L  N  M  O
A  O  I  J  R  T  Q  I  L  I  L  U  R  N
S  M  N  F  E  V  C  O  S  A  L  L  T  E
E  A  C  N  T  U  B  A  N  P  B  O  E  E
B  T  R  O  M  G  N  O  G  A  R  M  I  C
C  O  E  N  O  B  M  O  R  T  I  A  Y  V
C  C  A  S  T  A  N  E  T  S  C  P  H  C
```

121

PUZZLE 82: COMPOSERS

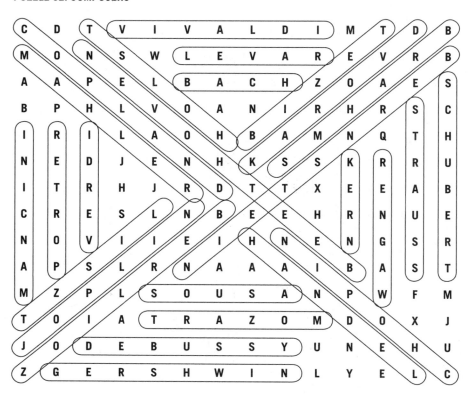

PUZZLE 83: BROADWAY MUSICALS

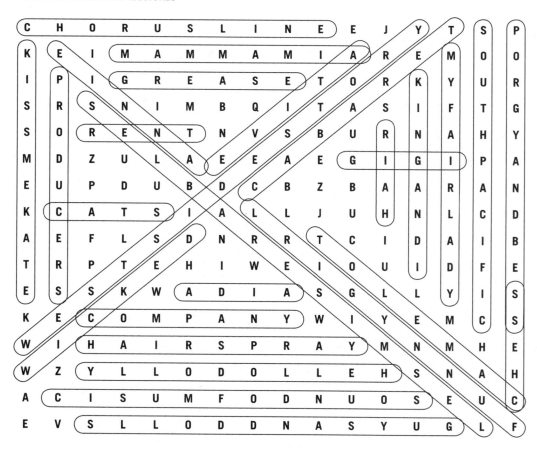

PUZZLE 84: ITALIAN MUSICAL TERMS

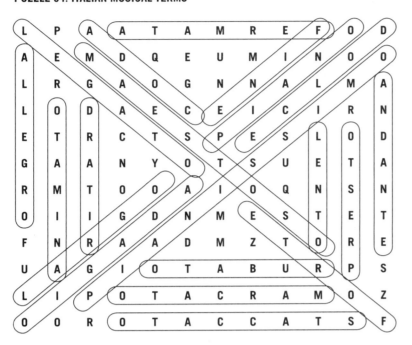

```
L  P  A  A  T  A  M  R  E  F  O  D
A  E  M  D  Q  E  U  M  I  N  O  O
L  R  G  A  O  G  N  N  A  L  M  A
L  O  D  A  E  C  E  I  C  I  R  N
E  T  R  C  T  S  P  E  S  L  O  D
G  A  A  N  Y  O  T  S  U  E  T  A
R  M  T  O  O  A  I  O  Q  N  S  N
O  I  I  G  D  N  M  E  S  T  R  T
F  N  R  A  A  D  M  Z  T  O  R  E
U  A  G  I  O  T  A  B  U  R  P  S
L  I  P  O  T  A  C  R  A  M  O  Z
O  O  R  O  T  A  C  C  A  T  S  F
```

PUZZLE 85: KINDS OF MUSICAL WORKS

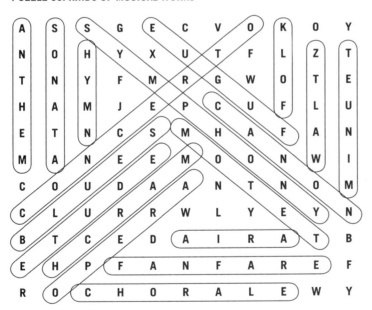

```
A  S  S  G  E  C  V  O  K  O  Y
N  O  H  Y  X  U  T  F  L  Z  T
T  N  Y  F  M  R  G  W  O  T  E
H  A  M  J  E  P  C  U  F  L  U
E  T  N  C  S  M  H  A  F  A  N
M  A  N  E  E  M  O  O  N  W  I
C  O  U  D  A  A  N  T  N  O  M
C  L  U  R  R  W  L  Y  E  Y  N
B  T  C  E  D  A  I  R  A  T  B
E  H  P  F  A  N  F  A  R  E  F
R  O  C  H  O  R  A  L  E  W  Y
```

PUZZLE 86: JAZZ LEGENDS

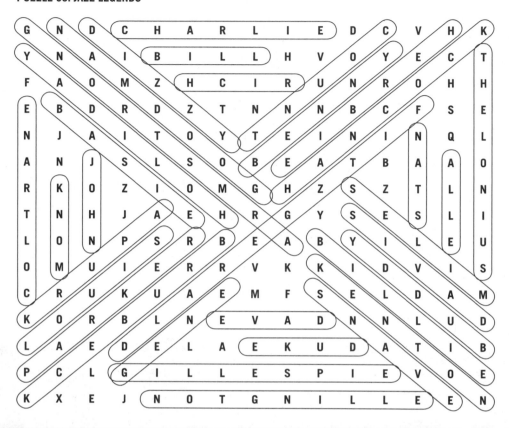

SECTION 10 - KRISS KROSS

PUZZLE 87: ITALIAN MUSICAL TERMS

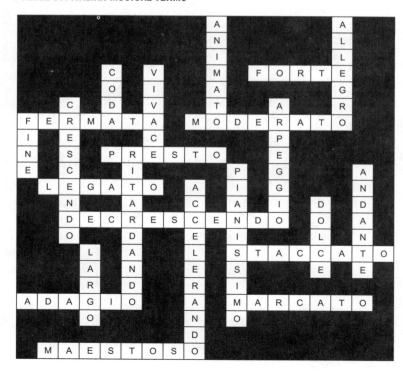

PUZZLE 88: KINDS OF MUSICAL WORKS

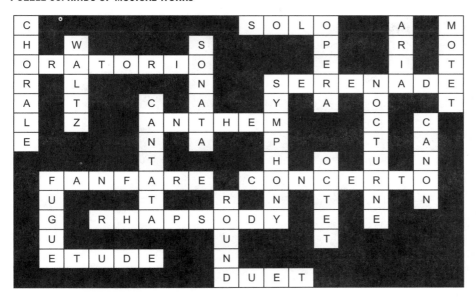

PUZZLE 89: COMPOSERS—NOW & THEN

PUZZLE 90: MUSICAL INSTRUMENTS

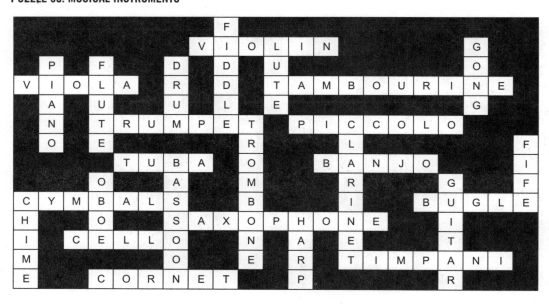

PUZZLE 91: BROADWAY MUSICALS

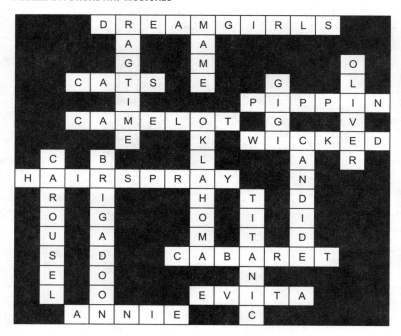

PUZZLE 92: MUSICAL TERMS

PUZZLE 93: THE ABE BRADY STORY

This is the story of (1)ABE Brady, a mythical lumberjack, and his great ox, (2)BABE. (3)ABE was so big that when his (4)DAD built a (5)BED for him it was as long as a soccer field and as wide as a (6)CAGE for 43 lions. The (7)EDGE of the (8)BED was so high that it took 102 sacks of ox (9)FEED to build the steps so (10)ABE could get into (11)BED at night.

(12)BABE wore a (13)BADGE with a (14)BEAD border, saying that he was not to (15)BE (16)FED any (17)CABBAGE, no matter how much he (18)BEGGED. You know, of course, that (19)EGG sandwiches and (20)CABBAGE were Babe's favorite foods.

One day, (21)ABE decided to take a trip. He called for a (22)CAB, which, because he was so big, needed to be the size of a truck. (23)ABE loaded his shoulder (24)BAG and (25)BAGGAGE, and then told the (26)CAB driver to take him to the (27)DECADE (28)CAFE, where the (29)FAB Four and the Grateful (30)DEAD were giving a concert.

After the concert, (31)ABE had a dinner which included (32)BEEF stew and biscuits with (33)BEE honey. He was so hungry that the cook (34)ADDED more (35)BEEF and vegetables. (36)ABE was still hungry, so he asked if he could have a (37)DAB of ice cream. Now for big (38)ABE, a (39)DAB of anything was enough to open a store. The ice cream was served in three wheelbarrows, each containing a different flavor. "(40)GEE," (41)ABE said, "Where is the chocolate sauce?"

(42)ABE was a lumberjack, which means he cut down trees. The best trees were on the (43)FACE of the mountain. (44)ABE did not want to cut down all the trees, so he had to (45)GAGE the (46)AGE of the trees and only cut down the most (47)AGED ones. His axe was so big that when he swung it, he chopped down 15 trees at a time. This made so much noise that even the (48)DEAF could hear the trees fall.

PUZZLE 94: THE TRIP WITH MY FATHER

For many years my father traveled on business trips. But I had never gone anywhere. "(1)GEE, (2)DAD, why can't you do a good (3)DEED and take me along? I just (4)ACED my math test, so this would be a great reward for me." I (5)BEGGED and pleaded, but it seemed as though he was (6)DEAF since he kept ignoring me. Then, with a grin on his (7)FACE, he said "Put (8)FEB. 21st on your calendar, and we will go.

When that day came, we loaded our (9)BAGGAGE into a (10)CAB and were off to the airport. On the plane, I was on the (11)EDGE of my seat with excitement. The only thing (12)BAD about the flight was that they didn't (13)FEED me anything but a (14)BAG of peanuts.

Once we landed, Dad took me to an outdoor (15)CAFE. They had lots of (16)EGG dishes on the menu, so Dad ordered an omelet. I ordered corned (17)BEEF and (18)CABBAGE. While we were waiting for our food, (19)DAD kept talking about the building with the beautiful (20)FACADE across the street. I was more interested in the nearby (21)CAGED parrot that (22)FACED me and tried to (23)GAB with me.

After we were (24)FED, we had a full day of touring. I went (25)GAGA over some of the sights we saw and things we experienced. At the end of the day, I couldn't (26)GAGE how many miles we had walked, but as the sunlight (27)FADED, even at my (28)AGE, I was (29)DEAD tired and (30)BEGGED to go to bed early.

NOTE: The letters in each block may appear in any order.

PUZZLE 95: BUILDING BLOCKS A

	BLOCK 1		BLOCK 2		BLOCK 3		BLOCK 4
1	A	1	L	1	T	1	O
2	N	2	E	2	Y	2	B
3	S	3	H	3	V	3	K
4	U	4	F	4	W	4	P
5	X	5	M	5	D	5	R
6	J	6	G	6	C	6	I

PUZZLE 96: BUILDING BLOCKS B

	BLOCK 1		BLOCK 2		BLOCK 3		BLOCK 4
1	B	1	A	1	N	1	D
2	R	2	M	2	U	2	T
3	L	3	E	3	F	3	C
4	S	4	O	4	P	4	H
5	K	5	J	5	V	5	G
6	Q	6	I	6	W	6	Z

PUZZLE 97: BUILDING BLOCKS C

	BLOCK 1		BLOCK 2		BLOCK 3		BLOCK 4
1	B	1	E	1	A	1	T
2	S	2	O	2	W	2	L
3	U	3	C	3	D	3	H
4	F	4	Q	4	V	4	I
5	P	5	R	5	Z	5	G
6	M	6	Y	6	N	6	K

PUZZLE 98: BUILDING BLOCKS D

	BLOCK 1		BLOCK 2		BLOCK 3		BLOCK 4
1	A	1	L	1	T	1	O
2	V	2	D	2	C	2	U
3	E	3	B	3	R	3	F
4	M	4	S	4	Z	4	P
5	N	5	H	5	G	5	Y
6	J	6	I	6	W	6	K

NOTE: For each puzzle, the answers on lines 1 through 4 may appear in any order.

PUZZLE 99: #1-4

1

A	B	C	D	E
B	R	A	S	S
C	OR	N	E	T
TR	U	M	P	ET
B	U	G	L	E
FR	EN	CH	HO	RN

CAT BRASS
1. CORNET
2. TRUMPET
3. BUGLE
4. FRENCH HORN

2

A	B	C	D	E
S	T	RI	N	GS
VI	O	L	I	N
C	E	L	L	O
GU	I	T	A	R
F	ID	D	L	E

CAT STRINGS
1. VIOLIN
2. CELLO
3. GUITAR
4. FIDDLE

3

A	B	C	D	E
WO	O	DW	IN	DS
F	L	U	T	E
BA	S	SO	O	N
SA	X	OP	HO	NE
PI	C	CO	L	O

CAT WOODWINDS
1. FLUTE
2. BASSOON
3. SAXOPHONE
4. PICCOLO

4

A	B	C	D	E
D	R	U	M	S
B	O	N	G	O
S	N	A	R	E
TI	M	P	AN	I
D	JE	M	B	E

CAT DRUMS
1. BONGO
2. SNARE
3. TIMPANI
4. DJEMBE

PUZZLE 100: #5-8

5

A	B	C	D	E
T	E	M	P	O
L	A	R	G	O
AN	DA	N	T	E
P	R	E	S	TO
A	L	LE	G	RO

CAT TEMPO
1. LARGO
2. ANDANTE
3. PRESTO
4. ALLEGRO

6

A	B	C	D	E
MU	S	IC	A	LS
G	R	E	A	SE
A	N	N	I	E
W	I	C	KE	D
HA	IR	S	PR	AY

CAT MUSICALS
1. GREASE
2. ANNIE
3. WICKED
4. HAIRSPRAY

7

A	B	C	D	E
DY	NA	M	I	CS
P	I	A	N	O
F	O	R	T	E
CR	ES	CE	ND	O
S	FO	RZ	AN	DO

CAT DYNAMICS
1. PIANO
2. FORTE
3. CRESCENDO
4. SFORZANDO

8

A	B	C	D	E
CO	MP	O	SE	RS
H	AN	D	E	L
B	I	Z	E	T
BR	AN	H	M	S
M	O	Z	A	RT

CAT COMPOSERS
1. HANDEL
2. BIZET
3. BRAHMS
4. MOZART

PUZZLE 101: MAZES - PIANO

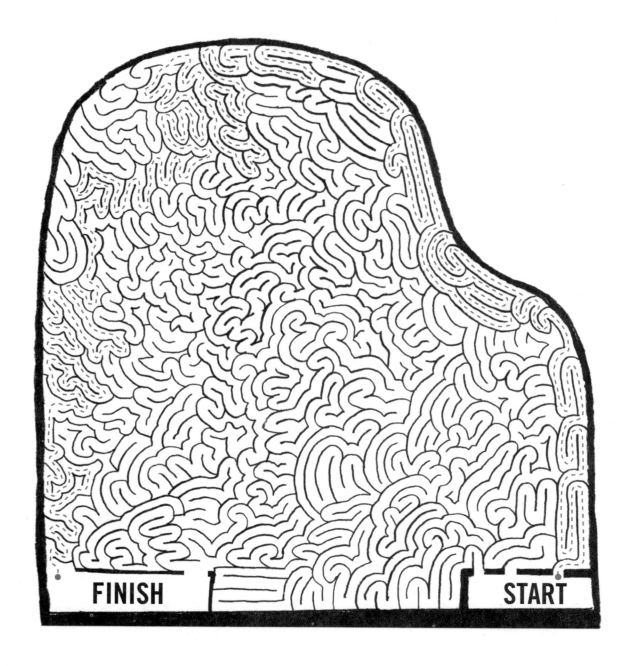

PUZZLE BONUS: MAZES - MARACAS

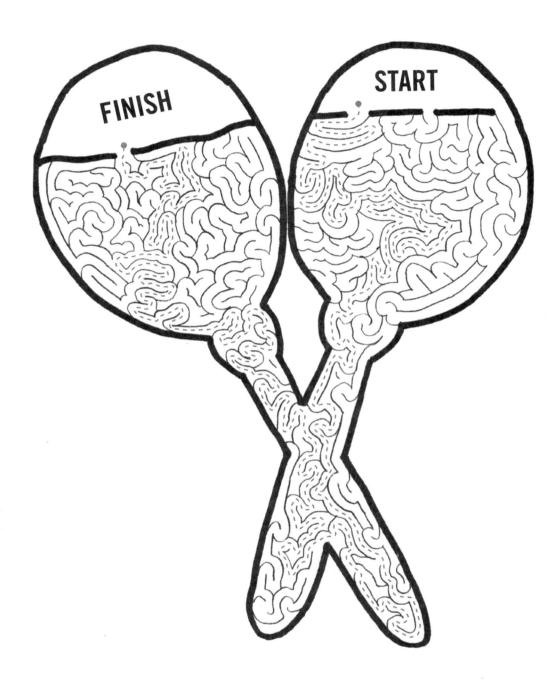

ACCENT ON COMPOSERS

The Music and Lives of 22 Great Composers
with Listening CD, Review/Tests, and Supplemental Materials
Jay Althouse and Judith O'Reilly

Accent on Composers is a 100% reproducible book with listening CD designed to introduce students to the lives and music of 22 great composers. It may be used, either as supplementary materials or as a specific curriculum, in a general music class or in a course in music literature or history. For each composer, students will study the life of the composer, then listen to a well-known and representative musical work by the composer. Recommended for grades 5 and up.

CD KIT (20048)

READY TO READ MUSIC

Sequential Lessons in Music Reading Readiness
Jay Althouse

Don't ask your students to read music until they are "ready to read music." This 100% reproducible book is packed with four sequential units of eight lessons each, all designed to prepare your students to read music. Most of the lessons are followed by a page of exercises, ideal for student assessment. And, as a bonus, there are page after page of large, reproducible music symbols...great for bulletin boards and flash card learning. Recommended for K-8.

REPRODUCIBLE BOOK (21835)

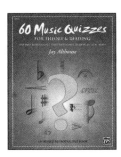

60 MUSIC QUIZZES FOR THEORY AND READING

One-page Reproducible Tests to Evaluate Student Musical Skills
Jay Althouse

Just what the title says: 60 one-page quizzes on a variety of subjects related to beginning music theory and reading. Includes sections on "The Basics," Rhythm," "Note Names," "Key Signature," "Musical Symbols and Terms," "Time Signature," "Keyboard Identification," and "Musical Puzzles." Perfect for student assessment. Recommended for grades 3 and up.

REPRODUCIBLE BOOK (27144)

MUSIC PUZZLES PLUS

25 Educational and Fun Puzzles for Classroom and Home Use
Donald Moore

Includes 25 music games and puzzles, word searches, rounders, "name that tune" games, word and geography puzzles, and crossword puzzles. Answer keys included. Recommended for grades 4 and up.

REPRODUCIBLE BOOK (23857)

Please visit our website **alfred.com** or contact your favorite music dealer for current pricing and availability.

Sue Albrecht Johnson received a bachelor's degree from Wittenberg University and a master's degree from Kent State University. She was a mathematics teacher for 25 years in the Cleveland, Ohio area. As an avid puzzle solver and developer, Sue incorporated many types of puzzles into her daily classroom activities. Sue received Teacher of the Year awards from both the Greater Cleveland Council of Teachers of Mathematics and the Ohio Council of Teachers of Mathematics. Besides presenting several workshops in the United States, she has shared her knowledge of teaching mathematics with educators in Ecuador, Colombia, Guatemala, Mexico, and Australia.

Sue has used her mathematics skills in a variety of ways. For the sport of Synchronized Swimming, she has been in charge of the scoring for the Summer Olympics in 1984, 1996, 2000, 2004, and 2008 as well as several World Championships and Pan American Games. She has served as the U.S. National Scoring Chair. In addition, Sue is in charge of the scoring for the US Open Golf Championships each year, as well as several other PGA Tour Events.

Music has always been another love. Besides singing in her church choir and university choir, Sue sang with the Cleveland Orchestra Chorus for 18 years under the direction of Robert Page.

Sue currently resides with her husband, Harry, in Manhattan Beach, California.